A Protestant Approach to the Campus Ministry

A Protestant Approach TO THE *Campus Ministry*

by

JOHN E. CANTELON

THE WESTMINSTER PRESS

Philadelphia

LIBRARY OF CONGRESS CATALOG CARD NO. 64-12142

PUBLISHED BY THE WESTMINSTER PRESS ®
PHILADELPHIA, PENNSYLVANIA 19107

PRINTED IN THE UNITED STATES OF AMERICA

To the staff
of the Department of Campus Christian Life,
in fond remembrance of the years 1957–1960,
this work is respectfully dedicated

Contents

✠

Preface

✠

We are living in a time in which many facets of the church's thought and life are being reexamined in the light of the worldwide social revolution, the new cultural situation, and the impact of theological and Biblical studies. Ecclesiastically everything seems to be up for grabs. Nowhere is this reappraisal more vital than in the area of religion and higher education, for it is here that church and culture confront each other in that microcosm of the world which is the modern university. It is in our colleges and universities where young men and women who will be the decision makers of the future are being trained, and where thousands who will guide the destinies of the so-called "newer nations" of the world are being exposed to American culture today.

The church must continue to rethink its understanding of its campus ministry in the face of this situation and its own responsibilities. This book is intended, not as a summary of a finalized theological position, but as a part of an ongoing dialogue in the intensely dynamic field of religion and higher education. Three primary concerns are reflected in this work. First, it is important that there be available in concise form a statement of the developing theology of the Protestant involvement in higher education for the use of university pastors, college chaplains, and their advisory boards and committees. A second concern is to provide a study book for discussion among faculty, administrators, graduate and undergraduate students, on the role of the church in higher education. A third purpose may be served to the degree that this work provides some understanding of the nature of the campus ministry for the increasing numbers of lay men and women in and out of the university who are concerned about the church and its role in higher education.

This book is the product of more than a decade's concern for and involvement with the campus ministry in a variety of positions — college town pastor, university pastor, Board Secretary, and university chaplain. The substance of the material herein set forth was prepared for staff training conferences for new university pastors of several denominations — The United Presbyterian Church in the U.S.A., the Presbyterian Church in the United States, the United Church of Christ, the Disciples of Christ, and the Evangelical United Brethren.

J. E. C.

Chapter One

✠

The Theological Context for the Campus Ministry

THE LATE DEAN INGE of St. Paul's once began a sermon at Oxford with the comment, "We live in an age of crisis [long pause], as Adam said to Eve as they left the Garden of Eden." The wry Dean then went on to attack one of his favorite enemies, crisis theology. His observations were probably necessary to correct a natural human propensity to see the problems of the present age in exaggerated terms. Yet there is much evidence to support the thesis that the first half of the twentieth century is one of the most critical periods in world history. The relative stability of the late nineteenth century with the rise of European empires under the sway of the *Pax Britannica* gave way in the twentieth century to a period of general Western cultural decline that has continued to this day. Despite the increased wealth of the Western powers, principally America, the balance of world power and the initiative in cultural creativity have moved out from under exclusive Western aegis.[1]

The result of this cultural movement has been a wave of uncertainty regarding the future of Western institutions, a failure of nerve that seems to infect every aspect of modern society. Such major periods of cultural decay and uncertainty in the past have frequently been, interestingly enough, times of unprecedented theological creativeness. Both the fourth and the sixteenth centuries witnessed the breakdown of traditional cultural forms and paved the way for new developments. And both of these centuries were periods of extensive theological activity. But one has to go back to these very same centuries to find ages characterized by as much creative theological ferment as our own. The modern ecumenical movement within Protestantism, Orthodoxy, and Roman Catholicism, the rise of Biblical studies and the production of great theological analyses and systems are all indications of this creativity. One may hazard the guess that, instead of living at the end of a period of cultural growth, we are poised at the very threshold of new and exciting cultural creativeness.

Of the many potentially creative developments in the life of the church in the mid-twentieth century, one of the least spectacular may have the most significant impact. Much has been made of the suburban religious revival that followed upon the Second World War and that only now shows signs of tapering off. Unprecedented numbers of Americans joined churches, and millions were spent on church buildings and educational units. There has even been evidence of an increased interest in lay theological study and a new zeal for ecumenical conversation and experimentation. These developments have had a good press. But another movement within Protestantism, which is most relevant for its ministry in the present age, has not been so widely recognized or acclaimed. This is the new Protestant involvement in higher education.

The period following the Second World War has seen the emergence of a totally new concept of the church's relationship to the field of higher education. A theologically mature philosophy of the mission of the church on the campus is being worked out. The contrast between this emerging philosophy and the one that previously prevailed can be seen most clearly from the perspective of a brief survey of the genesis and growth of the Protestant campus ministry. The earliest campus Christian ministry in this country was carried on in the period following the Civil War by the Y.M.C.A. At its inception this approach to the campus was strongly evangelical and farsightedly ecumenical. Through such cooperative agencies as the Y's and the Student Volunteer Movement, state schools and those private universities which had ceased to have denominational connections were penetrated by a dynamic Christian lay movement concerned with presenting the claims of the gospel to students and recruiting young men and women for the foreign mission field.

After the Y's became accepted as a part of campus life, it was natural, with their Christian concern for service, that they should look about for ways in which to aid the whole academic community. Thus there emerged an auxiliary conception of the role of the Christian community in higher education. Besides raising the sights of student concern in the establishment of settlement houses in disadvantaged sections of the large eastern cities, the Y was instrumental in the development of student counseling services, placement bureaus, and freshman orientation camps. Some of these functions became so significant in student life that the academic institutions themselves were motivated to take them over and operate them. The Y's thus fulfilled a necessary role in putting themselves out of business as the colleges and universities themselves began to do on a much larger scale what the Y's had sensitively initiated. During this period of increasing Y social service, the theological barrenness of the American Protestantism of the thirties took a heavy toll in the area of the Y's own self-understanding. The earlier clear Christian missionary vision tended to be blurred, if not lost, and the service programs of the community Y's became the dominant influence in their philosophy of operation. It was in the first decade of the twentieth century that many Protestant denominations began the development of their own campus movements, sometimes in cooperation with the Y, sometimes separately.

The conception that characterized these early denominational campus Christian fellowships was that of providing a "home away from home." Since not all of the church's youth did — or, for that matter, could — attend the approved denominational colleges, it was determined that something should be done to retain them for the church and preserve them from the vicious secularism of the state and private universities. The church determined to follow its youth to college, and its philosophy of the campus ministry was that of nurture.[2] Sometimes it bordered on protection. The churches built large fraternity-type houses near the campuses where student pastors lived with their families and the expanded family of students. At best this approach to the campus ministry provided a valuable service to a few lonely students, encouraged some to enter the ordained ministry, and freed able campus pastors to expand the concept of the ministry which was entrusted to them beyond the narrow confines of nurture. At its worst, however, it eventuated in the denominations trying to save students for the church by saving them from an education!

Since the Second World War, a new philosophy of the campus ministry has been developing among the principal denominations which, like the earlier Y ministry, is both missionary and ecumenical. The trend has been away from conservation of the church's youth in a nurture experience toward involving them in responsible witness in the university seen as a microcosm of the culture. No longer is the ministry seen as being related to the peripheral " auxiliary service " tasks of the university, but it is directed to the university's principal academic task. The stress is placed upon responsible studentship. The Christian in the university is called upon to learn to love God with his mind.

This shift from providing auxiliary services to meeting the intellectual challenge in higher education has meant that the role of the discipline of theology in the campus ministry has been greatly heightened. Those persons responsible for the campus ministry of the Protestant denominations have recognized that a contemporary witness in the field of higher education must be theologically oriented and undergirded. The campus ought to be the place where the best thinking of the church meets the best thinking of the culture.

Many developments make this encounter between theology and culture uniquely possible today. The almost unprecedented period of theological creativity which, as has been noted, can only be compared in importance to the Reformation era, is a most potent factor making for academic dialogue. But other factors have also contributed, some of which we shall be exploring later. The emerging ecumenical movement has expanded the frontiers of all Christian thought, and various lay-theological study movements have equipped nonprofessionals within the universities to be involved in relating Christian faith to various academic disciplines. It has been said that the challenge presented today to Christian students and faculty in the university is how they may be men and women of faith in the new world that is rapidly taking form (and for which the university is so largely responsible) as their fathers were men of faith in the world that God gave them. To meet such a challenge and task, God has provided and is providing new resources.

The development or reawakening of a dialogue between Christian faith and the academic disciplines raises the age-long question of the relationship between faith and reason. The problem of this relationship may be seen in terms of the issue of their continuity or discontinuity. If revelation, the unique concern of evangelical theology, is held to be so distinct an order of knowledge as to be totally different from, and unrelated to, other kinds of human knowledge, then no real dialogue may take place between church and university. No evaluation of revelation is possible and no criteria for judgment are available. On the other hand, if the continuity between reason and revelation is insisted upon, and revelation is treated as of a piece with other kinds of human knowledge, then revelation loses its distinctiveness and becomes a human creation or at least humanly controlled. Any attempt to relate theology and philosophy must deal with this vexing problem. A brief survey of the history of the relationships between these two disciplines will assist in understanding the nature of the dialogue that is beginning to go on today.

Both theology and philosophy in Western culture emerge out of a profound cultural synthesis, the interpenetration of Hebraic and Hellenistic cultures, which eventuated in what is known as Christendom. This synthesis has had worldwide significance because it could take into account more of human experience than any other cultural creation. From its Greek heritage Western culture learned to comprehend order, to deal with nature as the realm of necessity. And from its Hebraic roots it learned how to comprehend history, which is the realm of the unique in human experience, a curious compound of freedom and necessity. Each culture, Greek and Hebrew, was deficient in comprehending what the other could. Thus in the Western synthesis, both order and novelty, repetition and the exception, could be found meaningful.[3]

This Western cultural synthesis took place under ecclesiastical sponsorship and control. Philosophy and theology were related in such a way that theology dominated philosophy. Theology was known as the " Queen of the Sciences " and thereby earned the unenviable distinction of becoming the first imperialist among the academic disciplines. The role of philosophy became that of *ancilla*, handmaiden of theology. Thus theology found philosophy helpful in explaining her claims and clarifying her doctrines. Augustine used the Platonic philosophy as transmitted through Plotinus in his theology. But the great synthesis of Greek philosophy with theology was the creation of Thomas Aquinas, whose magnificent intellectual edifice crowned the Scholastic endeavor. Both Augustine and Aquinas might have justified their use of philosophy by noting that the apostle Paul in his letter to the Colossians had used early Gnostic ideas as the vehicle for the expression of his Christology. In any case, syntheses of one sort or another were formed between philosophy and theology, and one of these, the Aristotelian, gradually became dominant in Roman Catholicism, though not officially so until the last century.

It has been suggested that it is instructive to see the role of philosophy in medieval Scholasticism as analogous to the role of the servant in the modern upper-middle-class household. Many servants today do not " live in." Rather, they constitute what is known as " day help," coming from their own homes to serve in their employer's and returning home each night. So in the medieval synthesis philosophy was " day help " in the great temple of theology. Philosophy had an independence and autonomy of her own. She was no mere slave or chattel of theology. Or, to change the figure, she did not merely occupy an inferior niche in the Thomistic cathedral. Philosophy, as handmaiden of theology, had her own Platonic or Aristotelian home. What is more, theology for some time was not much concerned about what kind of philosophy performed the household tasks. Only very much later was it determined by the Roman Church that Aristotelianism was the only proper servant of theology.[4]

The sixteenth-century Protestant Reformation provided, as one of its unintentional side effects, an impetus leading to the liberation of philosophy from its servant role or bondage to theology. This was certainly not because the Reformers were academic liberals desirous of freeing captive learning. Rather, it was because they felt that the servant philosophy had gradually become dominant in the household of theology and had perverted the true nature and function of theology. As sometimes happens, the servants in a corrupt or degenerate household become the *de facto* masters. This, Luther felt, had happened in the medieval church. Philosophy, far from serving theology, had become a tyrant over it.

Luther's distinction between the order of creation and the order of redemption provided the opportunity and occasion for the beginning of the autonomy and integrity of the disciplines. This was one step in the gradual coming of age of Western culture as it began its independence from the mother church. Such maturation has been a long, slow process, filled with quarrels and tensions, as the church has often attempted to prevent the independence of culture, and culture " trialed and errored " its way toward autonomy, frequently misusing its newfound freedoms. Thus philosophy gradually became independent of theology, and, in time, various other disciplines split away from philosophy, finally getting some things settled, as it has been observed.

It is well known that the Reformers were heavily dependent upon Augustine. But they took issue with him in one very important matter. This was Augustine's identification of God with the Truth.[5] Augustine found this identification of *deus* with *veritas* helpful in relating the concerns of the Greek philosophers (*veritas*) with the passion of the Hebrew scriptures (*deus*). It also proved a nice little apologetic tool since it enabled one to argue against any serious disclaimer of the existence of God. For if one passionately denies the existence of God, he presumably does so in the name of truth. But if God and truth are one, then, in denying God, he is affirmed.[6] By identifying truth and God, the Scholastics had opened the door to the gradual dominance of philosophy over theology. The Reformers attacked this Scholasticism because it founded religion not only upon supernatural revelation, but upon natural reason. Calvin and Luther insisted upon the sinfulness of human reason. Like every other human capacity, they regarded it to have been infected and distorted by sin, that fatal *incurvatus in se,* the turning in upon oneself which uses all things to further the ego. What Freud has reminded modern man concerning his reason, that it is so often rationalization, the Reformers knew as they saw reason as a faculty used by the sinful self. Truth for the Reformers, the highest truth of which man was capable, was not rational information about the universe, but rather divine truth. This was the truth that grasped man and was not available to the philosophic mind. It was truth that had the initiative over man, not truth waiting passively for human discovery, nor being subject to human control or manipulation.

But developing Protestantism soon forgot the Reformers'

attack upon the simple identification of God and the truth. Protestantism in the seventeenth century developed its own brand of Scholasticism. Like the medieval Scholasticism that preceded it, Lutheran and Calvinist orthodoxy tended to define faith as intellectual assent to doctrines and revelation as the transmission of sacred data or truths. The Enlightenment happily accepted the Augustinian identification of truth and God, receiving added impetus from a forgetful Protestant orthodoxy. But the Enlightenment did not share orthodoxy's view of truth. Rational information about the universe became the important truth. Data tended to become truth, and therefore, God. Rationalism managed, with this weapon, to call most of orthodoxy's tenets into question on the very basis of orthodoxy's identification of truth with God.

It was Immanuel Kant who subverted the foundation upon which the identification of God and the truth had been based. If Kant were taken seriously, such identification would be impossible. Kant showed the impossibility of constructing a rational metaphysics. He rejected intellectualism, proclaimed the humility of reason, only to fall into moralism. But despite Kant's work and his commanding place in modern philosophy, the nineteenth century went on to identify God and truth.[7] No longer did philosophic truth bow to the superior revelation of God, as with Augustine. Rather, revelation was regarded as an inferior expression of philosophic truth, probably necessary because of the limitations of the common mind. The result of this identification of truth with God in the nineteenth century was to make a philosophy out of theology. Knowledge became, as Francis Bacon said it was, power. This even became power over God. *Deus* became subject to *veritas*.

The Reformers of the sixteenth century and Søren

Kierkegaard in the nineteenth had seen the dangers of this identification. God's freedom was limited. A certain amount of religious knowledge seemed to be a prerequisite for the establishment of a relationship between man and God. God was made dependent upon man's intellect for revelation. But Christian faith claimed the opposite. Paul wrote the Corinthians that " not many of you were wise according to worldly standards, not many were powerful, not many were of noble birth; but God chose what is foolish in the world to shame the wise, God chose what is weak in the world to shame the strong, God chose what is low and despised in the world, even things that are not, to bring to nothing things that are " (I Cor. 1:26-28).

Intellectualism and orthodoxy both erred in supposing that a mind filled with truths about God thereby had faith in God. Because it equated truth with God, it interpreted faith as agreement with external authority, subscription to doctrines. The identification of God and truth in the rationalist sense of that word imposed conditions upon God in his self-revelation. Today some existentialist theologians emphasizing the boundary-line situations seem similarly to impose crisis as the essential condition without which God cannot reveal himself.[8] Both this brand of existentialism and the older rationalism must be rejected in the affirmation of the freedom of the God revealed in the Biblical tradition.

Revelation, in the Biblical witness, is not the transmission of information or data. It is rather the establishment of a relationship, a fellowship. Revelation is personal, not conceptual. It is finding oneself confronted and addressed by a Thou. Certainty is not possible in dealing with God. God is free. This means that theology should not attempt to become a pseudo philosophy and pretend to describe that to which ultimate reality (God) must conform. The task of theology is rather to describe, *post eventum,* what God has done as this is transmitted by the Christian community, and to do so in terms of faith. It should not seek to become metaphysics or a higher type of philosophy.

The possibility is thus open today that theology need not be a cryptophilosophy, nor philosophy a cryptotheology. A genuine integrity and autonomy of the two disciplines may be affirmed. This does not mean that tensions between the two disciplines will not arise. But it does mean that such tensions will not consist in the denial of the other discipline's right to exist. Members of each discipline may now recognize what they have in common, the same logic, the appeal to the same basic human experiences, as well as what separates them — philosophy being concerned with general truths, while evangelical theology limits itself to the elucidation of one particular message. Both philosophy and theology may attempt to understand what the other is saying, without seeking to modify, let alone discredit or destroy it. An openness to the other discipline would tend to make the normal tensions of their relationship fruitful.

The place of philosophy in the modern American university is certainly far from its traditional dominant position. Since the beginning of this century no single philosophical school has dominated the university to provide a unified framework for all the disciplines. Indeed, philosophy illustrates the cultural confusion of our era noted earlier. The current prominence of linguistic analysis in American schools of philosophy underscores the abdication by philosophy of its once-dominant position as the new Queen of the Sciences. Most linguistic analysts are content to ply their logic-chopping trade solely in order to provide the natural sciences with more efficient linguistic tools and make no pretense at the construction of a unifying meaning system.

In this situation it may well be the task of theology to support philosophy in her traditional role as the synoptic discipline and thereby to assist in the rehabilitation of the university in one of her more significant tasks, that of universal critic of culture.

Philosophy, however, cannot alone be the sole concern of theology in the university. The modern college cannot and should not return to some idealized past where philosophy was the chief focus of study. The dominant place of the natural and social sciences in modern higher education reflects the new society in which the university lives and which it must seek to serve. This means, among other things, that theology cannot be content to see its task restricted to the treatment of the traditional reason-revelation problem.

Another and more adequate way of looking at the theological context for the task of the campus ministry in our time is to see it as a part of the major issue of the relationship between religion and culture. This is the broadest aspect of the faith-reason problem. It has the advantage over the narrower formulation of the problem in seeing the issue in the total context of a complex cultural situation. If the campus is, as it is so frequently called, a microcosm of the world, then the relationship between Christ and culture becomes a highly significant expression of the problem the church faces in the field of higher education. As helpful as it has been to see the task of the campus ministry in terms of the age-old philosophical and theological issue of the relation of faith to reason, an even more valuable way of stating the problem may therefore be in terms of the relationship between church and culture. It is to this formulation of the problem that we now turn.

Chapter Two

✠

The Problem: The Relationship Between Christ and Culture

A prominent strain in modern theology has assisted the Protestant churches in seeing their philosophy of the ministry in higher education as part of the greater issue of the relationship between Christ and culture. As we have noted, the Christ-culture phrasing of the problem has the advantage of removing the issue from the narrow philosophical problem of the nature of religious truth. It insists that we see the university in the setting of its total relationship to culture or society and opens the door for an appreciation of the changes that history has brought about both in the role of the university and in the role of the church.

Casting the issue in terms of the Christ-culture problem directs attention to the most widely circulated work dealing with this issue in the English language, *Christ and Culture,* by the late H. Richard Niebuhr.[9] In this book Niebuhr accepts a broad definition of culture as all that which is acquired by man beyond the biologically given. Culture thus is something learned and therefore every culture requires the existence of education in one form or another. In the West the university is one of culture's most significant expressions. One might say that the university is the place in our society where Christ and culture confront each other most directly. Since the university tends to lead the culture around it by some twenty years in terms of discoveries and attitudes, this means that the church's ministry in the university is highly important as it portends the significant issues some years before they become generally encountered. Experiences of the church in the area of higher education thus have an important place in the whole area of church-culture relationships.

In *Christ and Culture,* H. R. Niebuhr sets forth five types of relationship between Christ and culture: radical opposition, fundamental agreement, Christ above culture, polarity between Christ and culture, and Christ converting culture. The first two may be dismissed as setting forth an understanding of the relationship between Christ and culture that classical Protestantism has never and can never accept. Only a radical fundamentalism could take seriously the position of Christ totally opposing all of culture. Niebuhr reminds us of the impossibility of separating men from their culture. "Christ chooses no man purely as a natural being, but always as one who has become human in a culture, who is not only in culture, but into whom culture has penetrated."[10] The diametrically opposed position that sees Christ and culture in fundamental agreement has also no historical roots or ideological appeal to those who stand in the tradition of the Reformation. This position of complete synthesis removes the offense of the gospel which cannot be removed. It fails to appreciate the judgment upon all of human culture that Christ makes. Both of these positions, radical agreement and disagreement, involve a rejection of theology, Niebuhr notes, but for different reasons: "They [the synthesists] reject theology, as the radicals do, although for the opposite reason; since the latter regard it as an intrusion of worldly wisdom into the sphere of revelation, and the former believe it to be irrational." [11] The theological preoccupation of classical Protestantism makes it uncongenial to these two positions at opposite ends of the Christ-culture spectrum.

The position of Christ-over-culture is that officially represented by the Roman Catholic Church. It might also be said to represent the relationship between Christ and culture accepted by some Episcopalians. The primary limitation of this position is that it leads to an absolutizing of what is inevitably relative. Niebuhr claims that " the effort to bring Christ and culture, God's work and man's, the temporal and the eternal, law and grace, into one system of thought and practice tends, perhaps inevitably, to the absolutizing of what is relative, the reduction of the infinite to a finite form, and the materialization of the dynamic. It is one thing to assert that there is a law of God inscribed in the very structure of the creature, who must seek to know the law by the use of his reason and govern himself accordingly, but it is another thing to formulate the law in language and concepts of a reason that is always culturally conditioned." [12] This is a succinct statement of the classical Protestant critique of Roman Catholic natural law.[13] Historical reasons for the development of this position will be noted later as well as reasons why it is not an option for contemporary Protestant theory even if there were an actual possibility of putting it into effect.

The two relationships between Christianity and culture that are feasible for contemporary Protestantism are those labeled " polarity " and " conversionist " by Niebuhr. The polarity position is one particularly identified with the Lutheran tradition. The characteristic insight of this position is that man is the subject of two loyalties, both of which make valid claims upon his life. The order of nature and the order of grace comprise the two spheres in which obedience must be lived out. But these orders are not only discontinuous, they are largely opposed to each other. The Christian lives in a state of constant tension between the two. Thus the Christian must speak continually in paradoxes. He is sinner, yet justified, a believer who doubts, assured of God's salvation, but walking the knife edge of insecurity. For him in Christ all things have become new, and yet everything remains as it was from the beginning.

There are obvious Biblical roots to this position. Niebuhr credits those who have held this position with faithfulness to at least a major segment of the gospel. But he also shows his predeliction for the conversionist position when he credits the polarists for making inadvertent contributions to culture. It was this polarity relationship which made for the autonomy of the academic disciplines, at least in theory. The church regarded as the sphere of redemption has no special insights into the proper ordering of the sphere of creation. But in practice, the church still exercised a dominance over the disciplines in the universities and colleges under ecclesiastical pressure or control.

Although he is sympathetic with this polarity relationship between Christ and culture, Niebuhr is also quite explicit as to its limitations. He points out that it is open to convenient rationalization so that economic exploitation and the most cynical forms of political theory may be justified by appeal to it. The polarist may end up either in a virtually antinomian attitude toward society or in an implacable conservatism. Human institutions are regarded in a negative fashion as merely dikes against sin rather than "positive agencies through which men in social union render positive service to their neighbors advancing toward true life." [14] The most incisive attack on the polarity position is the one made from within the Lutheran tradition itself by Dietrich Bonhoeffer, who points out that thinking in terms of two spheres assumes that there are realities which lie outside of the dominion of Christ. Insisting on the objective, all-inclusive nature of God's act in Jesus Christ, Bonhoeffer rejects the polarity position as bifurcating reality and challenging the supremacy of Christ. He writes, "There are . . . not two spheres, but only the one sphere of the realization of Christ, in which the reality of God and the reality of the world are united."[15] Furthermore, the polarity position regards history as essentially a static border warfare between Christ and world rather than history being drawn into Jesus Christ who is its center and meaning. It is Bonhoeffer's contention that the whole Protestant ethical theory has been damaged by this thinking in terms of two spheres. It is for this reason that he undertakes a revision of the classical conception of the orders of creation — family, labor, state, and culture — treating them positively rather than negatively as mandates of Christ rather than structures for the prevention of the spread of sin. The background and import of Bonhoeffer's thinking will occupy our attention following some necessary comments on Niebuhr's fifth relationship between Christ and culture, termed the conversionist position.

As has been noted, this position is the one obviously favored by Richard Niebuhr. Here Christ is seen as the transformer of culture. A more hopeful and positive attitude characterizes this view of man's culture. History is seen as a dramatic interaction between God and man. Niebuhr cites the Fourth Gospel, some of the letters of Paul (principally Colossians), Augustine, and Calvin as proponents of this view. Both Paul and Augustine succumb to a more negative viewpoint bordering on, if not actually being, dualist in the end. Niebuhr is puzzled by Augustine's failure to develop the full implications of the conversionist position. Perhaps this is to be explained by the particular social and political situation of Augustine's time. The Roman Empire was being shattered by the barbarian invasions just after the church had won acceptance by the Empire. Such events could not but lead to a pessimism regarding the structures of this world more akin to the polarity position than the conversionist.

The danger in the conversionist position is that it may slip easily into a Christ-over-culture attitude on the part of churchmen. It is essential that the church be aware of Christ's Lordship over the world as well as in the church and that his relationship to the world is not dependent upon or limited to the church. God's judgment and mercy are active beyond the boundaries of the church, although it is through the living witness of the church that the world may know whose judgment and mercy are at work in it. The position, to be clearly understood, must be regarded as emphasizing Christ and not the church as the converter of culture. The church, like the university or any human institution, may be used by Christ, but it is not his sole agent for conversion. The conversionist position finds history profoundly significant as the sphere in which God is active, and the church's role in history becomes the clue to understanding the meaning of history itself.

As has been indicated, the contemporary Lutheran martyr Bonhoeffer represents most clearly a conversionist position with respect to the relationship between Christ and culture. But to comprehend the background of Bonhoeffer's thinking here, it is necessary to turn to a theologian who had great impact on the attempt to understand history as being at the heart of Christianity.

Although somewhat out of fashion until recently as a left-wing liberal, Ernst Troeltsch has made a great contribution to the understanding of the church-world issue. Trained by Ritschl in the need for a grasp of the historic, Troeltsch went far beyond Ritschl in his attempt to find what history meant.[16]

In his two-volume work, *The Social Teaching of the Christian Churches,*[17] Troeltsch took up the problem of trying to understand how it was that the church was involved in social issues. Writing at the end of the nineteenth century in Germany, Troeltsch found that among other voices expressing opinions on a variety of social issues, there is the voice of the church. Troeltsch would like to have evaluated the effectiveness of these social pronouncements, but he did not have, nor could primitive sociology still in embryonic form give him, the tools necessary for such an evaluation. But what also fascinated Troeltsch was that the churches had become involved in this field at all. He, therefore, undertook a historical study of the social teachings of the churches. What he had begun to see was that if Christianity is historical in nature (as Ritschl and Harnack seemed to establish), then if he could understand how the church, in its history, became involved in the world, he would have a clue to understanding Christian thought as a whole. The history of the church's relationship to culture then became a paramount problem. The church's position with respect to the world was the key to the whole of Christianity.

Troeltsch found that in antiquity Christianity had no social teachings in the proper sense of that term. The world outside the church had no enduring significance. That world was believed to be passing away soon. The Second Coming of Christ was imminent. Thus the early church could see no reason for social reform. Hence there is no condemnation of slavery as an institution, although there are teachings regarding the attitude between Christians who happen to be masters or slaves. But between the time of the early church and the Middle Ages, Troeltsch noted, a profound change had taken place. This change might be described as a fusion between Christianity and culture in such a way that Christianity came to dominate culture.

Thomas Aquinas, for example, had an explicit political theory in a way that Augustine had not. Between these two men there had developed a fusion or intellectual interpenetration between church and world. Troeltsch also saw that this meant that the Reformation was dependent upon this fusion. If there had not been a Thomas Aquinas, there would never have been a Luther or Calvin. For the Reformers did not reject the medieval question regarding the fusion between church and world; they merely rejected the Roman Catholic form of this fusion. Like the Scholastics, the Reformers presumed the existence of the *corpus Christianum,* the coterminal state and church.

The test case for Troeltsch was found in the difference between Western and Eastern Christianity. The Orthodox Christianity of the Eastern world never experienced this same fusion which, indeed, took place in the West for a very specific set of historical reasons. In the Western part of the Empire, after the beginning of the barbarian invasions and with the removal of the capital to Constantinople, the only institution left that spanned the past and present was the church. The Western church, under papal dominance, took seriously, as part of its work, a civilizing activity that the church never had before. It became responsible for education and law, for the form and content of society in general. In this mingling of interests, the medieval Catholic outlook took form. Christendom was the product of this activity.

The *corpus Christianum* was conceived and the whole sociological order was brought under the dominance of Christian thought. Protestantism presupposed this fusion. Indeed, without it the Reformation would never have taken place, as it did not take place in the Eastern church. In Eastern Orthodoxy new religious points of view developed strictly along individualistic lines. Tolstoy is the good representative of protest movements within Eastern Christianity.

It is against this background of the fusion of Christianity and culture, in what Niebuhr has termed the Christ-above-culture position, that the Reformation took place. It is also from this same background that the modern world begins to emerge in the period of the Enlightenment. The Western world at this time gradually threw off the shackles of church dominance. The Reformation contributed to this process only indirectly in breaking the monolithic unity of Catholic culture. Troeltsch noted that Puritanism has been the only thoroughly worked out Protestant equivalent to the Catholic fusion of religion and culture. We are, in mid-twentieth century America, living in the time of the waning of the last significant impact of Puritanism upon culture. This means that the last church-culture fusion is rapidly losing its influence on the culture, no longer even being something for youth to protest as it was in the twenties.

The modern world insists on understanding itself in its own terms, not in ecclesiastical terms. Thus the situation of the church today is, in some respects, like that of the early church. But the church today has a heritage that the early church did not have — that is, an explicit doctrine of the world in a world that does not recognize Christianity as dominant. It is at this point that Dietrich Bonhoeffer's insights become vitally important. Much has been said about his trenchant little phrase, " The world has come of age." [18]

This phrase is found in Bonhoeffer's writing when he is talking about the way in which history emerges only after Jesus Christ. Bonhoeffer notes what Troeltsch had seen so clearly, that Christianity and Western civilization grew up together. He saw clearly that what was happening in our present day is that Western civilization was being factored out into its original components: the *corpus Christi* (the church) and the world. But the modern world cannot be understood apart from this background. Bonhoeffer writes: "The epoch making events of history affect the whole of the West. The unity of the West is not an idea but an historical reality of which the whole foundation is Jesus Christ. The fact is that the kind of rejection of God which is present in the complete autonomy of the Enlightenment would not have ever been possible had the fusion of Christianity and civilization not at one point taken place." [19]

Now the implications of Bonhoeffer's insight are momentous. Not only does it assist in our understanding the past history of the West, which is unintelligible without a knowledge of Christianity, but it also helps determine the future relationship between the church and the world. For while Bonhoeffer would surely say that this medieval fusion was good and essential for the fulfillment of God's purposes in history, it is certainly the height of folly to try to return to the medieval or Puritan pattern. Just as adolescence is a necessary stage in the movement from childhood to maturity, so the medieval synthesis was good, but now "the world has come of age."

It should not be the church's task to try to reestablish control over the world. Rather, the church should recognize that it has a unique opportunity today — that of being free to stand in the world and argue that it is not in terms of some predominantly ecclesiastical civilization, but rather in terms of the awareness of God himself, that the world can become what it really was meant to be. What this meant for Bonhoeffer was that a genuine secularism was possible. With respect to the issue of the church and the university, this means that the church should not seek to dominate educational institutions, but rather enter into dialogue with them in order that, on the university's own terms, it may become what God intended it to be.[20]

What may be called Bonhoeffer's conversionist position is informed by the significance of historical developments. Indeed, awareness of the movement of history that has produced the fusion and fission of church and culture assists in a modern appreciation of a doctrine of the Holy Spirit. It may be contended that the Christian has a positive view of change because change is the clue to the next movement of God the Holy Spirit in history. This certainly is the nature of the prophetic tradition in which the prophets stood firm when all men were panicked by the future, for despite the tragedies of history it is still the locus of God's judgment and mercy. Thus the Holy Spirit may be viewed as the agent of change in the historical dynamic.

If one understands Bonhoeffer correctly, the church, despite its increasing alienation from the modern world, need not despair. Rather, it may have a positive attitude toward the world and its culture. Because it is aware of the leading of the Spirit in its past history, it dares hope for the future. Because it believes that Western history has its roots in the historical experience of Jesus of Nazareth and that this same Western history is determinative in the whole of world history, the church may yet view the "secular" world in positive terms. In its unparalleled modern situation, the church must therefore bring itself to the support of a true secularism, rather than hoping for the return of some particular ecclesiastical synthesis that gave it status or dominion in the past.

This newly found position with respect to the church's attitude toward the world must also be applied to its relationship with that world in microcosm, the university. What the church must seek is an autonomous university, freed to be itself, fulfilling the critical function that properly belongs to it. The church must seek to support this integrity of the university against those forces which would seek to pervert it.[21]

The church today is challenged to relate itself as a servant to the university, which is suspicious of the church because of its dominance of the university in its historical past. The university is sometimes naïve about other forms of domination and may fall captive to alien powers that blunt its critical function. It is the church's task to fight against these powers and for a truly secular institution free from all special interest.

The fulfillment of the new creative role of the church within the university is dependent upon the existence within the university of a theologically articulate laity, trained and supported by ordained clergy who have a clear vision of their own role in this specialized ministry. The task, also, is of such a nature and magnitude that only a cooperative ecumenically oriented approach can hope to make any impact upon the expanding educational scene. An understanding of the corporate ministry of laity and clergy in an ecumenical context is, therefore, a necessary prerequisite to the implementation of the church's mission in higher education.

Chapter Three

✠

Ecumenical Ministry and the Role of the Laity

There are, broadly speaking, two divergent conceptions of the role of the laity of the church. On the one hand, the laity's function is thought of as essentially supportive. The structure, theology, and mission of the church are the primary concern of the clergy, with the laity giving part-time assistance to the full-time work of the ordained ministry. Nurture and loyalty are the key words in this conception of the laity's ministry. The clergy nurtures the laity in their life of faith, keeping them close to the church's institutions and busy with its varied functions. The laity are expected to exhibit loyalty to the denomination, supporting its programs, fulfilling its quotas, refurbishing its fabric.

On the other hand, there is an emerging conception of the role of the laity that sees their function as the leading edge of the church's essential mission of the world. Here the function of the ordained ministry takes on the supportive characteristics usually associated with the laity. Ministers' pastoral and teaching functions are directed to the end of the " equipment of the saints, for the work of ministry " (Eph. 4:12). In this conception vocational evangelism and corporate obedience are key words. In vocational evangelism the stress is upon the layman's worldly vocation as the significant frontier between church and world where the gospel must be proclaimed. In corporate obedience the stress is upon the continuing consideration by the whole people of God of its response in the structures of society to the Christ who is the Lord of the whole earth. When mission is viewed in these terms, then such a contemporary statement of the same problem as the one we have explored by Richard Niebuhr becomes highly relevant.

Whichever of these two basic concepts of the role of the laity is taken, radical implications for the conception of ecumenical relations follow. If the supportive role of the laity is the operative one, then ecumenism becomes only an option for those who are interested in that sort of thing. Since attention is focused primarily upon the support and upbuilding of the denomination, ecumenical relations are not central — indeed, they may be ultimately a grave threat to the whole churchly enterprise.

Since, at the present time, the dominant view of the role of the laity is a supportive one, it may be maintained that whatever impetus there is in ecumenical relations among American denominations derives its force from other than theological factors. Both the general drive for togetherness in an increasingly other-directed society and the movement toward institutional consolidation, which marks this particular phase in the development of capitalism, may be cited as key forces in American ecumenism. Of course, there are lay men and women as well as clergy who are convinced of the central place of the ecumenical movement for good and sound theological reasons, but these are, by and large, a minority — though hopefully a creative one. But the general lifelessness and artificiality of the ecumenical movement represented in local councils of churches indicates that whatever its mainspring may be, it is far from the dynamic centers that are spawning church buildings and constructing vast church programs for thousands of suburban Christians across the land.

Now, if the role of the laity is seen as the frontline shock troops of the Christian mission, then the stance toward ecumenical relations changes dramatically. The primary concern shifts from the denomination and its programs to the society and the world into which the church is sent. And neither society nor the world is organized denominationally. This is the crucial factor in mission and the key to genuine ecumenical involvement.

Once, we know, society was arranged, for the most part, denominationally. At the time of the Reformation in Europe, national, state, and regional churches expressed the mission of the church catholic to the particular area, culture, or society in which they lived. But the conception of a basically Christian culture, expressed in terms of the *corpus Christianum* inherited from medieval Roman Catholicism, vitiated whatever missionary vision existed in the Reformation churches. Nurture under the benevolent aegis of a well-established and well-educated clergy, and close cooperation with the civil authority, all but obscured the missionary thrust of the gospel in the world. The role of the laity in the reformed churches remained supportive almost to the same degree as within Roman Catholicism.

This picture was complicated when the European national churches were transplanted to America. But for some period during the early colonial days, the European situation was viable with different Protestant groups being identified with specific geographical areas. As the nation grew, transportation improved and the dynamic of American culture began to demonstrate its heterogeneous character, and a relatively new situation emerged. With no denomination established by law, with church membership but a small percentage of the total population, the fiction of a coterminous state and church could no longer be maintained. Various racial, religious, and national groups lived side by side in the same communities, so the "patchwork quilt" denominational pattern of Europe became a sort of "shot silk" pattern in this country that defied limiting association only with members of one's own religious group. Indeed, the survival of the American experiment in nationhood depended upon cooperation across what were before primary barriers of race, language groups, and religion. In such a situation any naïve indiscriminate proselytism could not survive and the church had no other concept of mission in society. Not being quite sure how to conduct themselves, the churches began to concentrate upon nurture of their own membership and revival campaigns directed toward the uncommitted within the country. Lay activity was more and more enlisted for the support of the denomination. Indeed, with the many denominations to keep up and with the growing programs by which the denominations hoped to maintain their relevance in a secular society that increasingly performed what were formerly church functions (hospitalization, education, social relations), the laity had little time or energy for mission!

In this situation premium tended to be placed upon the marginal differences between denominations, largely those of organizational structure and liturgy. Thus the inward life of the denomination became strengthened, while the outward life could be expressed only in terms of the foreign mission enterprise and those special areas of concern where the denominations either historically or constitutionally had been unable to operate along traditional lines.

It is interesting to note that it was from two of these

areas — foreign missions and the Student Christian Movement — that laymen brought back into the church the concern for mission and unity that lies at the heart of the ecumenical movement. As is well known, the nineteenth-century foreign mission enterprise, which enlisted lay men and women on the same basis and pay as the ordained clergy, was the instigator of the worldwide ecumenical movement. Denominationalism, nurture-minded and non-missionary, raised no ecumenical problems at home. But this same denominationalism, vibrant and mission-minded abroad, found itself face-to-face with grave ecumenical issues. It was discovered that the gospel just could not be given a particular denominational label and that the divisions of Christendom, so easily accepted at home, were a scandal to both non-Christian and the newly converted abroad. It must be admitted that the comity arrangements that were worked out as a solution to this problem were and are exceedingly imperfect answers to the basic question. Comity merely is an attempt to impose the " patch-work quilt " European pattern, and it results in effectively removing ecumenical involvement by geographic division and separation.

Student Christian movements and the Y.M.C.A.'s, as we have already noted, were early forms of an ecumenical campus ministry. The denominations could cooperate to some extent with these organizations because state and private universities were virgin territory in which the denominations were at a loss how to function. Again, laymen and laywomen involved in the life of the university led the way to a new conception of mission which was strongly ecumenical by its very nature. There is significance in the fact that both of these movements — foreign missions and the student Christian movements — were organized, for the most part, outside of the churches. The denominations were too rigid, too suspicious, and too preoccupied with their own institutions to provide the freedom for such movements to develop within them.[22]

The relationship between the lay ministry and the changing morphology of the ecumenical movement is a fruitful area for some speculation. Although the original impetus of the ecumenical movement came, as we have noted, from the foreign mission field, its initial expression in the Western churches was what is called the Life and Work Movement of what is now the World Council of Churches.

In this phase of ecumenical development little or no stress was placed upon theology, attention being directed to the area of good works in which Christians could cooperate regardless of denominational differences. Lay participation in the Life and Work Movement was significant, as its focus was the world in which the laity were already involved. But because of its naïve avoidance of theology, confessionalism, and denominational heritage, the Life and Work Movement failed to fill a dominant role in the life of the churches.

The Faith and Order Movement, preceding, and now within the World Council of Churches, is a much more respectable form of ecumenical encounter as far as the denominations are concerned. It deals with theology and polity, both of which lie at the heart of the church's self-understanding. It was and is also primarily a movement of professional theologians, although it enlists the support and interest of some lay theologians as well as those who have had experience and training in the student Christian movements and foreign mission field.[23]

Although it is recognized that the Faith and Order Movement has contributed much to the maturity of ecumenical relations, and will continue to have its place in all future ecumenical developments, its growing professional requirements and focus of attention upon the church rather than upon the world makes it unlikely that it will continue at the forefront of ecumenical relations. Although it is much too early to make even a speculative judgment, it would seem at least possible that a movement having its origin in the student Christian movements may hold promise for future ecumenical progress. This is the Life and Mission emphasis of the World's Student Christian Federation. Based upon certain needs and problems of the student movements found to be worldwide in scope, but also upon Visser 't Hooft's observation that for the first time since the Reformation we have a Protestant concensus on the nature and mission of the church, this movement may combine the world-centered aspect of the Life and Work Movement together with the theological maturity and perspective represented in the Faith and Order Movement.

Just because it focuses upon the world into which the church is sent, the Life and Mission emphasis involves the laity as absolutely essential to its existence. And resting upon the developing Biblical theology that most Protestants share, the dynamic behind the concern for mission is not a humanistic compassion or a Christian pietistic concern for the individual, but a solid theological awareness of the peculiar role which the church is called upon by God to play within the world. If the Life and Mission emphasis succeeds in its task of radically transforming and energizing the student Christian movements, then there is good hope that the power of its life will increasingly be felt in the life of the churches in the years to come. Together with other numerous experiments in lay ministry, the Life and Mission emphasis may play a significant role in developing an increasingly powerful and mature lay ministry within the world.

Our current understanding of the ministry of the church, especially as it is engaged in mission in the field of higher education, may therefore be summarized under ten major points:

1. There is only one essential ministry and that is the ministry of Jesus Christ. All other ministries are subordinate to, dependent on, and derivative of, his Messianic ministry. The life of the church, as the whole people of God, is a continuation of this one Messianic ministry. And, as T. W. Manson has noted, this means "its continuation *by the Messiah*. The Body of Christ is the organism that he uses to carry out his purposes in the world in the same way that he used his physical body in the days of his ministry in Galilee and Judea." [24]

2. The apostolic ministry, so closely related to the earthly ministry of Christ, was unique and is definitive for the church. William Wolf states: "The apostles and their immediate followers actually share in the great events of Christ's life and teaching, his death and Resurrection, his Ascension and Pentecost. Their successors can never achieve direct participation in these revelatory acts in history. Therefore there is a normative quality about this primary community of response that cannot in the same degree attach to later and dependent periods of Church history. There is a transition from the Church as an organic part of God's revelation to the Church as a channel or primary instrument for the mediation of this revelation." [25]

3. Our understanding and evaluation of the contemporary ministry of the church must be in terms of the one Messianic ministry revealed in Scripture and participated in so directly by the New Testament church. This means that

minority status, failure in the world's terms, and a continual rhythm of death and resurrection characterize the true expression of the Messianic ministry rather than the morphology of growth proper to all natural institutions. In Luke's Gospel, Jesus pointed to healing, recovery of sight, resurrection, and the preaching of the gospel to the poor as validating marks of the Messianic ministry. (Luke 7:18-23.) This means that the effectiveness of the church's ministry should be judged in contemporary terms according to its power to exercise a healing, reconciling role in the world, and to convey insight and vision which illuminates the reality of the human condition. The church's ministry should be judged by the extent to which it gives its life for the world, experiences the power of God's resurrection, and manifests God's concern for the dispossessed and oppressed.

4. The ministry of the whole people of God is characterized by an "Israel element" and a "Christ-event element." The Israel nature of the church represents its continuity and the organizational form so necessary for any directed expression of community life. The Christ-event nature is the spontaneous, judging, shattering, reconstituting power of Christ as he gives himself to this people who are his body.[26] Within the total ministry of the people of God, there are specialized ministries derived from the special gifts wherewith Christ endows his body. Within these specialized ministries there is a particular ministry specifically related to the edification of the church. This particular ministry, historically related to the preaching of the Word and administration of the sacraments, is given by Christ as a guarantor of the continuity and catholicity of the church. It thus falls within the Israel element of the church, although it has often been open to the renewing power of Christ's reformation of his body. However, historically this

professional ministry has frequently hampered and, at times, almost obscured the charismatic ministry of the laity. Both ministries are, essentially, parts of the one ministry of Christ. Thus any church that elevates one of them above the other or virtually eliminates one is guilty of dividing the witness of the one body.

5. The situation that the church faces in the world modifies the form, but not the nature, of the one Messianic ministry that preserves, conveys, and lives out the message of the gospel. The fact that Jesus Christ is Lord of the world, whether it recognizes his Lordship or not, means that the world is not godless. Nor does the church have a monopoly on Christ's power or sovereignty. The church does not carry Christ into the world, but rather meets him and identifies him as Lord as it goes into the world where he is acting in judgment and mercy.

Dietrich Ritschl, of Pittsburgh Theological Seminary, has pointed out that the church differs from other human institutions in that its dynamic — the power that makes it what it is — is not focused just at its center, but is present actively at its periphery. The church, therefore, does not need to retreat into the fortress of its own life in order to find its Lord. But it finds him as it moves out into the world where he is reigning. This makes it imperative that the church learn how to "discern the spirits," i.e., take with great seriousness the task of judging which developments in the contemporary world scene are of God and which are not. The forms of the church's ministry, then, are not provided alone by strict adherence to internal tradition or established polity, but are developed in a dynamic relationship to the Lord who acts in the world.

Those who set forth what is known as a contextual or koinonia ethic as the form of Christian obedience in the world have shown that the situation or context of ethical action is itself ethically significant. Ethics is not a matter of merely applying ethical principles to a passive situation. It rather consists in discovering the living Word which constitutes obedience to the gospel in the particular situation. There is, therefore, a certain creativity in every ethical act. As Paul Lehmann has written of this ethic, "It regards what God has done and *what God is doing* as determinative of the ethical situation." [27] In like manner we may say that the world contributes something to the forms of the church's ministry in the world. Changes in culture and society or ministries to specialized groups in society must affect the form of the ministry.

6. There are two primary forms of the church's life, that of the gathered community and that of the scattered community. The ministry of the professional clergy has been primarily concerned with the church as the gathered community. This is natural, for the professional ministry must serve the essential tasks of the gathered community, as it (*a*) rehearses the mighty acts of its salvation in worship, (*b*) rediscovers its nature as the "sent people" through the sermon and study centered around the Word, and (*c*) plots the strategy of the people of God in the world. But, in concentrating on the upbuilding of the church as an institution, the professional ministry has obscured the form of the church as scattered in the life of the world. Yet it is the scattered form of the church's life that is the most significant, for it is in the world that the church performs its essential work of mission through witness. The church properly comes together as a gathered community only to further its task as the people scattered in the world.[28]

In the scattered ministry the work of the laity is more crucial than that of the ordained clergy. Therefore, the ministry of the clergy in the gathered church, both in its form and content, must be directed to the end of assisting the laity for their ministry in the world. The form of the gathered church must always be dependent upon the form of the church as the scattered Messianic community giving its life for the life of the world.

7. An ambivalent attitude toward the organized, gathered church is essential on the part of both clergy and laity. Because of our understanding of the mission of the church and the necessity for continuing reformation, we simply cannot accept the ministry of the church as it is commonly understood by most clergy and laity today. Since the rhythm of death and resurrection is determinative of the nature of the church's life, we must see the task of the renewal or rebirth of the church as providing the primary focus of the ministry of clergy and laity alike. The renewal of the church historically has always begun with the rediscovery by a creative minority of the shattering and reconstituting power of the Word of God as found in Scripture. The concept of the faithful remnant, preserved as much as is humanly possible from the pride that tends to characterize such groups, must be given tangible expression in the life of the church today.

The primary attention of the professional ministry must be given to this minority group and through it to the world. At the same time the organized church cannot and should not be rejected. To do so would be to yield to the prideful temptation of forming an ecclesiastical elite and to be cut off from the life, means of grace, and judgment that Christ has given over to his whole church whether it be disobedient or not. For it is the church that is the God-given agent for the proclamation of the gospel to the world. Groups that despise and cut themselves off from the life of the whole church soon lose their distinctive Christian message and wither.

It is, therefore, necessary to exercise careful judgment to discover how much time and energy should be given to the total organizational life of the church, knowing that, given our contemporary American situation, all the efforts of the professional ministry can be expended on just the housekeeping duties of the institution with none left for working with the creative minority in their spontaneous task of renewal. There must be a firm conviction on the part of this minority that it is God's intention that a self-conscious expression of the body of Christ take form in the midst of the natural communities of the world, and that Christ has given and will continue to give the gifts necessary for the work of the ministry to all who will faithfully follow him.

8. Within the ministry of clergy and laity there must be room for both spontaneous and intentional activities. The ministry of the clergy will probably always be characterized by more intentional activities than that of the laity. Both detailed plan and openness must be present if we are to carry out a ministry having continuity and focus as well as one open to the leading of the Holy Spirit. The almost exclusive emphasis on intentional activity within the gathered life of the church, with virtually no attention given to spontaneous witness in the world, makes it necessary to examine stringently and cut down ruthlessly the amount of planned church activities.

This does not mean that long-range planning ought not to be a characteristic of the ministry of the whole people of God. A systematic yet flexible plan for the extension of the ministry in every facet of society must be worked out by those who accept responsibility for the common ministry. It is especially true in specialized ministries that unless this tentative plan is the evaluative instrument, this ministry will be misunderstood by the whole church and judged by a host of criteria foreign to the essential nature of the ministry.

9. What is going on in the world is of the greatest significance to the form of the church's ministry in the world. Perhaps the most significant thing that is going on, at least in the Western world, is, as we have noted, the final breakdown of Christendom, that curious Greek-Hebrew amalgam which so long has dominated the world and may even be said to have created history.[29] Christendom is being factored out into its constitutive elements, the secular world and the Christian church. We should not reject this development since the synthesis was a rather artificial one, obscuring the church's mission in the world. For the first time since the Constantinian settlement, we are beginning to be able to experience the meaning of the church's real relationship to the world. It is certainly not our task to rebuild Christendom, as much of it as we can, or in any form to reestablish the hegemony of the church over the world.

Since we cannot rule the world, our task as Christians is not, as we seem to suppose, to fight the world. Rather, we must fight for the world, on behalf of the world. We ought to support movements toward a real secularism and aid everything that makes for the independence and integrity of the world. As Karl Heim has written: "The messengers of Jesus were called atheists (*atheoi*). They deprived the world of its gods, in order to prepare a place for the living God. In the present situation Christians should follow the precedent of the early Church: they should join those who deprive the world of its gods and who oppose all man's attempts to claim for himself and for his world the eternity and absoluteness which belong to God alone. In other words, *contemporary Christians should support those who relativize world and man.*" [30] It is not the witness of the church that *it* has united God and man, Christ and culture, but that we witness to One who is God and man and who has been made Lord of both church and world. In Jesus Christ and him alone are God and man, world and church all one.

10. It is of great importance that the church discover how to relate its ministry to the problems of the contemporary world and the present generation. To do so, many experimental specialized ministries of a great variety of types ought to be undertaken. Each of these experiments ought to be informed by this type of thinking concerning the ministry of the church. Only bold action along these lines will constitute the radical obedience demanded by the Christ who is shattering and rebuilding the world of which he is Lord and that is destined to be his eternal Kingdom where he will reign and into which shall be brought the glory and honor of the nations.

Chapter Four

✠

A Brief History of the University

There is interesting potential in following a line of thought stemming from Troeltsch with his deep appreciation of the historical nature of Christianity and modified by Bonhoeffer with his profound theological insights. This line of thought would indicate that the relationship between church and culture is the dominant factor in the growth of Western society. The problem of the synthesis or separation of religion and culture is the key problem for Christianity in every age. A reading of Troeltsch reminds us that the fission of the cultural synthesis dominated by the church is the great fact of the age in which we live and it must be the context in which the church carries out its mission in the modern world. Bonhoeffer helps us to take a positive view of this new role of the church in a secularized world. For the first time the church may serve the world without succumbing to the temptation to set up a predominantly ecclesiastical civilization.

Both Troeltsch and Bonhoeffer affirm movement in history. It is this movement which has produced the modern world. The Christian can take a positive attitude toward this movement because change is the clue to God's next movement and history is the setting for the action of the

Holy Spirit. This is no naïve historical progressivism that views events as bringing about an automatic increase in human goodness. In Bonhoeffer's case, at least, it was a faith like that of the Old Testament prophets who stood fast when everyone else fled. In Bonhoeffer's life, this faith produced responsible involvement in the great events of his time. Translating this faith into terms of the problems of the church's ministry in higher education would seem to require a sensitive appreciation of the history and development of the modern university in order that the church might be informed as to its responsibility for this changing institution with which it has been associated for so long. Indeed, a brief history of the university reveals much about the fission and fusion of religion and culture in Western civilization.

It is well known that what is known as the university had its roots, but not its direct historical lineage, in the Greek peripatetic schools of the seventh through the fifth centuries B.C. In these informal family-type associations, a sage and his disciples lived together, manifesting a particular way of life based on their conception of the universe and man's place within it. Contrary to some modern impressions, these Greek schools were not characterized by detached, objective attitudes toward their subject matter. The philosopher and his followers were free to think and inquire not because they lacked any convictions, but because they had a commitment and intense loyalties that gave them ground on which to stand and from which to explore man and his world. It was in these early Greek schools that the selection and division of subject matter was made which has persisted to this day. The liberal arts curriculum traces itself back to the trivium of grammar, logic, and rhetoric, while the sciences find their origins in the quadrivium of arithmetic, geometry, astronomy, and music.

There is no historical continuity between these Greek academies and the universities of western Europe. The Greek schools died, partly through the process of general cultural disintegration and partly because no general synthesis of their learning with the early Christianity was possible. The monastic schools of the early Christian era were not really embryonic universities, but provided only vocational training for the priesthood. The real succession from the Greek schools must be traced through the universities of the Muslim world where the Greek heritage was preserved and a high level of learning flourished long before the Western universities came upon the scene.

The university was a product of medieval society, that synthesis of religion and culture which occurred under the dominance of the Roman Church when it took up in earnest its "civilizing" task. The three traditional roles of Christ — Prophet, Priest, and King — became the basis for three major institutions that together created Western culture. The state exercised the kingly function of government; the church, the priestly function; and the developing university was to be the inheritor of the prophetic, judging, critical task so essential to society.[31] The dominance of the papal church over the two other institutions continually upset the balance of power in Western society, but the theory of a balance between the three institutions is important, especially in our time when the dominant institution tends to be the state.

The origin of the medieval universities was in the cathedral schools where the greater concentration of clergy provided the opportunity for informal tutorial arrangements to develop between the clergy and the sons of the nobility.[32] The cathedral school was the *studium generale* and it granted the license to teach anywhere — the *facultas ubique docendi,* from which phrase the term "faculty" developed. The curriculum in the *studium generale* was very informal at first. Alcuin of Tours (735–804), the scholar of Charlemagne, is credited with the introduction into the West of the Hellenistic trivium and quadrivium.

The term "university" came from the guilds and referred to one basic interest like that of the carpenters or chandlers and not to the breadth of subject matter explored. Papal charters were granted to some of these early institutions, and administrative functions began to be delineated, with a resultant increase in the security if not the autonomy of the faculty. The colleges developed later than the universities, but gradually came to dominate them, the universities tending to become a loose federation of colleges after the pattern of Oxford or Cambridge. The colleges, endowed by wealthy merchants, prelates, and the nobility, developed along the line of guilds of foreign residents in the cities who banded together for protection from the townspeople. Town and gown warfare is almost as old as the university in the West.

The thirteenth century was the golden age of Scholasticism. In this era the universities of Paris and Oxford came to preeminence. It was then that Aristotelian thought, preserved in Islam, was introduced to the West, becoming one of the major facets in the great synthesis of Christian and Greek philosophic thought in the works of Thomas Aquinas. This period of intense creativity, which saw the rise of the mendicant teaching orders, was succeeded in the fourteenth and fifteenth centuries by a period characterized by excessive formalism and the rise of nominalism. The Renaissance and the Reformation brought the third period of Scholasticism to a close and witnessed new changes in the universities. There was a revival of interest in the ancient classical languages, and, in Germany, investigation and research began to take priority in some universities over the function of transmission of cultural mores. The university began to be defined by its research function.[33]

The Reformation produced further changes in the university, but not as many as might have been expected. Calvin's Geneva Academy, founded May 29, 1559, despite some influences from Sturm's progressive academy in Strasbourg, was essentially built on Scholastic foundations.[34] The Academy was divided into two schools, a *schola privata,* a kind of prep school, and a *schola publica,* for advanced students. In the lower school there were seven forms, or grades, where subjects in the following order were studied: grammar (learning to read and write), French, introductory Latin, followed by more Latin, grammar and readings from Vergil, introduction to Greek, further Latin with readings from Cicero and Ovid, advanced readings in Cicero, Vergil, and Caesar, Greek readings in Homer, Xenephon, and Polybius, dialectic and rhetoric stressing the orations of Cicero and Demosthenes. Certainly the emphasis was not on the Biblical tradition to the exclusion of the classical!

In the upper school, students attended twenty-seven lectures a week: eight in Hebrew and Greek, five in the orators and poets, five in dialectic and rhetoric, three in ethics, three in physics and mathematics, and three in biology. In essence, this was good classical, Renaissance education. Frederick Eby writes of the Academy: "The success of the school and academy was amazing. During the first year 900 young men enrolled from all the nations of Europe. The institution was immediately recognized as the nursery of Protestant preachers and teachers for France and other lands. It was taken as the model for the organization of the University of Leyden in Holland, Edinburgh in Scotland, and Emmanuel College at Cambridge University, which in turn influenced the founding of Harvard in Massachusetts. Wherever the Calvinistic faith was carried, it aroused extraordinary zeal for education."[35]

In other Reformed countries emphasis was placed on the breadth of education for all classes and both sexes. In Scotland, John Knox proposed in the First Book of Discipline that every parish should have a school, every town a gymnasium, and every city a university. The money to finance this first complete national educational program was to come from confiscated monastic endowments. The rapacity of the nobility, who had already appropriated much of these endowments for their own uses, precluded the carrying out of this brilliant scheme.

The tradition of higher education in America, for so long under the dominance of Harvard University, also owes much to the Dissenting Academies set up by the Puritans in England after the Act of Uniformity of 1662 prevented non-Anglicans from teaching in the ancient universities. These Dissenting Academies began as theological schools, but ended up giving instruction to others as well. They had encyclopedic curricula much in advance of the older British universities of their day. At Kibworth Academy, for example, the four-year course included geometry, algebra, trigonometry, conic sections, physics, mechanics, chronology, Latin (which was used for all lectures), Greek, Hebrew, French, logic, disputations, rhetoric, oratory, civil history, ethics, metaphysics, theological disputations, Christian evidences, architecture, and military science.

The early American colonial colleges were patterned explicitly after the English models, particularly that of Emmanuel College at Cambridge. In organization, degree requirements, student life and discipline, the Puritan English pattern was imported, just as in the late nineteenth century American graduate schools patterned themselves after the German universities. The Harvard curriculum became basic for other American colleges.[36] The core of studies was the so-called "Greats" of the ancient British institutions, with the emphasis on classical languages, history, and literature. Added to this core were courses borrowed from the Dissenting Academies: Aramaic, Syriac, Hebrew, ethics, politics, physics, mathematics, botany, and divinity. This basic Harvard curriculum remained unchanged for well over one hundred years! English language, literature, and modern foreign languages were introduced by 1765. There were no electives, and the primary focus was on education for the ministry. As in the English universities, any graduate would automatically be granted his master's degree three years after he obtained the bachelor's.

Scientific developments and the nation's growing needs eventuated in new types of institutions in the nineteenth century. Rensselaer Polytechnic Institute was founded in 1824; in 1847 the Lawrence Scientific School was founded at Harvard, and about the same time the Sheffield Scientific School was begun at Yale. The land-grant colleges were established under the provisions of the Morrill Act of 1862. This event was decisive for the future of higher education in America. No longer was the church-related college or the private university to provide the dominant pattern for higher education. These land-grant colleges, the forerunner of the vast state educational systems of today, offered courses in the sciences, mechanical arts, and agriculture. But the liberal arts were not entirely omitted, and the programs tended to follow the pattern of the older Eastern colleges. The modern "political university," to use Sir Walter Moberly's expression, teaching democratic living and providing almost free higher education for all, constituted a unique American contribution to the history of higher education in Western culture.[37]

But coincident with the development of applied and technical colleges was the expansion of denominationally related institutions. These colleges were very conservative in their educational pattern. They were geared to provide a Christian ministry and to combat the secular influences of the rising state universities. These church-sponsored institutions have had an exceedingly high mortality rate. Among five hundred such colleges established before the Civil War, 80 percent did not survive. However, in the United States today over seventeen hundred liberal arts colleges are or were church-related. New ones continue to be founded every year.

The nineteenth century saw widespread curriculum development as well as expansion. The elective was a nineteenth-century invention. In 1825 the University of Virginia had eight schools: ancient languages, modern languages, mathematics, natural philosophy, natural history, anatomy and medicine, moral philosophy, and law. The student could choose his school, but not the courses within it. In the same year Harvard took a radical step. It permitted upperclassmen to take a limited number of electives. This was a very small chink in the curricular armor, but no further step was taken for forty years. In this same year, 1825, Yale took a retrogressive step. A report was accepted that defended the formal disciplines on the erroneous theory, not discredited until the twentieth century, that difficult subjects of no pertinence in themselves are of value because they strengthen the mind. No changes in the Yale curriculum appeared until the time of the Civil War.

Dr. Charles William Eliot, president of Harvard from 1869 to 1909, is noted for what has been called his " doctrine of election." Under his administration, initially required courses were limited to the freshman year save for rhetoric, philosophy, and political science. By 1883 three fifths of the freshman courses were electives. This laissez-faire academic system produced an increasing tendency toward specialization as few students elected courses unrelated to their particular vocational objectives. The phenomenon of broadly educated undergraduates began to disappear. In 1909 when A. Lawrence Lowell assumed the presidency of Harvard, a change was made and students were forced to study more broadly.

Little change in academic curricula occurred from the beginning of the century until the period shortly before — and at an accelerated pace since — the Second World War. The increasing emphasis on scientific and technical education brought about a concern for the humanities and the advent of core courses in the history of Western civilization. Also, the tremendous advances in the scientific disciplines, where new data produce changes almost every year, have brought about a stress on teaching a methodology rather than a particular content. These changes, together with others shortly to be explored in our examination of the crisis in higher education, have brought about a radical re-examination of curriculum in our day. Almost every major institution of higher learning is engaged in curriculum study and revision. It is not possible to predict the full nature of the outcome of this period of intense study and experimentation. But it is safe to predict that the university of the last half of the twentieth century will be as radically different from that of the first half as the university of the last half of the nineteenth century was from that of the first half. The question is whether the church will have exerted any major influence upon the thinking that will shape higher education and through it the world of tomorrow.

Chapter Five

✠

The Crisis in Higher Education

KARL BARTH has compared the impact of his " radical " theological enterprise upon the field of theology to a man stumbling about in the dark who grabs on to a line to support himself only to discover that he has taken hold of the rope to the town alarm bell. Soon the entire community becomes aware of him and his problem! The professional educator today often finds himself in a somewhat similar position. Searching for answers to the pressing problems of education, as he has been for a number of years, he has suddenly found an unaccustomed response on the part of the community at large.

Never before in American history has there been such widespread awareness of the crisis in the field of education. Concern is manifest for every aspect of the educational enterprise, from the primary school with the issue of " Why Johnny Can't Read " through college and university education to postdoctoral training.

Analysts of the crisis generally cite at least three underlying causes for it. The first, and most obvious, is the unprecedented numbers of young men and women who are seeking entrance into colleges and universities. The tidal wave of the post-World War II baby boom is about to inundate the campuses of our nation. This increase in the numbers of those of college age has been accompanied by an increasing percentage of those in this segment of the population who actually do seek a higher education.[38] Facilities in existing academic institutions will be taxed to their limits in the next few years despite frantic efforts in many places to anticipate the phenomenal growth. Junior colleges and four-year colleges are being established every month; teachers colleges are being turned into universities; and yet the estimated need far exceeds even these herculean efforts. A problem of particular concern is the vast increase needed in faculty to staff these institutions. Much is being done in experimentation with television teaching, trimester plans, and expanded programs for providing teaching assistants to meet the demand. Certainly there is little hope of being able to provide the number of qualified teachers in the traditional proportion to the number of students.

Were the crisis of numbers the sole major problem in the area of higher education, it would still tax our best resources to meet the challenge presented. But the logistical problem of numbers is only one reason for the crisis in higher education. The crisis in numbers, long foreseen and underscored by educators, did not focus public concern on higher education in anything like the dramatic fashion that the launching of the Russian Sputnik did in the autumn of 1957. Suddenly there seemed to be a realization of the necessity to catch up with, and attain the lead over, the astonishing Russian technical advance. This led to a reappraisal of the whole American educational picture. Whereas the crisis in numbers did not center attention on needs other than the need for increased gifts or tax outlays for buildings and faculty, the competition with Soviet education called the whole American educational process into question. Theory, goals, methodology, and curriculum were analyzed, argued, debated, and defended. High school principals took on admirals, and congressmen made invidious comparisons between the formerly sentimentalized American " little red schoolhouse " and the " big Red school system " of the Soviet Union.

The increased amount of attention being given to the teaching of the natural sciences, due to this concern about Soviet education, has caused alarm among the proponents of the liberating humanities. Those in the liberal arts have become concerned that the modern university is in danger of being transformed into a mere technical school. Other educators point out the danger of the dimunition of the traditional critical function of the university in society, since institutions of higher education sometimes regard themselves and frequently sell themselves to the public as instruments for the national policy, particularly in the area of national defense. Thus increased attention is being given to the relationship between the humanities and the natural sciences. The crowds that gathered in American universities from coast to coast to hear C. P. Snow lecture on this relationship attest to the level of concern in this general area. There has certainly been an increasing awareness that the smattering of courses in the field of the humanities injected into an otherwise altogether scientific or technical program is not a truly significant solution to the problem.[39]

The crisis in scientific education occasioned by the ascension of Sputnik has many ramifications in the third crisis area, that of curriculum. As we have seen, the curricula in use in many universities were developed over four decades ago and, in most respects, are based on concepts much older. Society and its needs have changed considerably in this period, and so have students. The amount of extracurricular, or to use the modern term, "cocurricular," activity on the part of students was considerably greater than it is now. It has frequently been noted that the amount of human knowledge doubles approximately every forty years, and this factor, together with increasing specialization, has led to the necessity for greater concentration in the various fields of study. Because of the crisis factors already noted — the competition of numbers, and the sense of imperative brought about by the emphasis on scientific and technical training — today's students are motivated to engage, are capable of being engaged, and must even of necessity engage, in the educational process in ways differing from previous generations. Colleges and universities are therefore challenged to revamp curricula and educational methods to take this new type of student into account.[40]

All of the reasons cited for the crisis thus far — population increase, scientific competition, and the changing student constituency — are certainly significant factors in the current educational crisis. They are mutually related and will continue to remain with us as pressing problems. None of them, however, goes to the heart of the crisis in education. The basic issue in American higher education is even more radical and perplexing. It lies in the fact that there is no agreement as to what higher education is in our society. Another way of stating the problem is to say that education is in crisis because there is today no generally accepted definition of the university. This might seem, at first sight, to be an overstatement. However, an increasing amount of evidence is available to support it. One may select this evidence almost at random from any sensitive report on education in our day. Take the article reported under the heading of "Times Topics" in *The New York Times* of November 13, 1957. This article states: "At almost any meeting of the

Poetry Society of America it is possible to start a near riot by propounding the simple question, 'What is poetry?' Similarly, among professional educators an exciting catch-as-catch-can mental wrestling match can be incited by asking ingenuously, 'What should be the major aims of American education today?' To the latter question replies would come chiefly from those who are concerned about our technological progress as means of survival and from those who are worried lest the liberating humanities be neglected in an overall plan. Scattered voices here and there would also remind us of the need for 'harmonious development,' 'spiritual inheritance,' 'economic preparedness,' 'habit inculcation,' 'complete socialization,' and other objectives long familiar to faculties and students of teacher-training institutions." The article goes on to note that the debate among educators reveals the lack of unanimity regarding the nature of the educational process in a day when some common understanding of the role of education is desperately needed. The very same issue of the *Times* also contained the text of the report to the Association of Graduate Schools. This report of the Committee on Policies, chaired by Dr. Marcus E. Hobbs, of Duke University, states: "We must ruefully conclude that the Ph.D. is tortuously slow and riddled with needless uncertainties; that it is frequently inefficient and traumatically disagreeable to the bewildered and frustrated candidate. The basic flaw is: We have never cleanly defined this protean degree." The report indicates that something as basic to higher education as the doctoral degree, the key to academic accreditation, lacks clarity of definition. Further evidence of basic confusion could be cited on every side. A comment, perhaps apocryphal, is attributed to Dr. Robert Maynard Hutchins, who, after noting in a lecture the complexity of the term "university," was pressed to define it by a member of his audience. The former Chancellor of the University of Chicago protested, stressing again the complexity of the term, but in exasperation finally said, "A university is a community to keep young men and women from worse places." The remark, though outwardly flippant or merely amusing, contained within it a basic insight of the problem of understanding the nature of the university. The university is very difficult to define!

The purpose, as is well known, behind the massive Harvard report *General Education in a Free Society* [41] was the attempt to delineate some cohesive factors for American education. This report states the problem very explicitly: a supreme need for American education is for a unifying purpose and idea. Some doubt may be expressed, however, as to whether the Western cultural ideal cited by the report is a sufficiently clear or unified concept to fulfill this supreme need.

Any study of the history of the university shows that this institution has fulfilled very different roles in the course of its development. These roles have been dependent upon some reigning concept of education — medieval, Renaissance, social democratic. Behind each of these concepts of education lies a view of man. As the "Times Topics" article cited above indicates, "Perhaps intelligent laymen can best guide their thinking not so much by what educators favor or do not favor as by reviewing the changing roles of the individual in different historic epochs." It is true that behind every university system there lies a theory regarding the nature of man. Education is always the attempt to form man according to some human ideal. Once this is seen clearly, then the root of the contemporary crisis in higher education may also be seen. It lies in the fact that contemporary American society is undecided about a specific human ideal; hence the crisis. The crisis, then, points to something deeper than the problem of numbers, or scientific versus humanist education, or curriculum revision. The crisis reflects the lack of a coherent image of man in our society.

The university crisis is thus a part of a general cultural crisis. This is the point that Dean Schilling, of Pennsylvania State University, makes when he writes, " In my opinion it is largely meaningless to apply the word *crisis* specifically to the university unless we mean simply that the world is in crisis or that the society of which it is a part is in crisis."[42]

This analysis of the crisis in education as centering in the problem of understanding the nature of man is shared by many thinkers in our society. Christians, Jews, and humanists see the problem focusing at this point. A reading of Christian theology may provide at least two profound insights here, making us aware of a difficulty in working out a solution to the vacuum caused by the lack of any explicit image or images of man, and carrying the analysis one step farther than a nontheological position would be capable of doing.

First, Christian theology would remind us that man is an ambiguous creation. He is undoubtedly the " knowing animal " who must be involved in self-knowledge, but he can never know himself completely. Man cannot make himself in his own image because he is made in the image of God. Thus he cannot be defined simply in his own terms or in purely natural terms.

As John Calvin observed, the knowledge of man is reflexive of the knowledge of God.[43] If man is to be known, he can be known through the God who created him. Man's attempts to define himself in his own terms only lead to a distortion of man. On the one hand, man may overstress his intellectual capacities and ability to transcend nature and thus distort his relationship to creation. He may think of himself more as an angel than as a human being. On the other hand, man may define himself entirely in natural terms, seeing himself as completely subject to the forces of nature, his glands, or his environment. In this case man chooses to understand himself as ape rather than as angel. These definitions not only distort the complexity of the human image (a dynamic combination of ape and angel) but they also have a way of becoming tyrannical ideologies whose proponents attempt to stifle whatever in man does not fit into the proclaimed definition.[44]

According to Christian theology, man is not to be comprehended merely by a set of ideas. He is a personal creation of God, and when the fullness of human nature was revealed to man, it was not in terms of a theology or an ideology, but in the Word made flesh. The mystery of humanity is preserved in the Biblical view of man, and an understanding of Christian faith ought to prevent us from ever trying to penetrate man's nature fully. The Greek maxim, "Know thyself," should be balanced by the Biblical insight, "O Lord, thou hast searched me and known me!"[45]

Thus any attempt to solve the crisis in education by calling an academic congress of philosophers, educators, or even theologians to delineate a contemporary American image of man would, from a Christian point of view, be disastrous. The view of man that would emerge from such a congress would inevitably be a distorted one and could be subject to demonic uses. What is desirable is a dialogue between varying views of man within active university communities. Such views of man are best embodied in living communities of commitment rather than in abstract formularies. This is one aspect of the relevance of communities of faith within the community of learning. Varying understandings of man should be presented, and commitment to these varying ideas of man ought to be elicited. But the formulation and imposition upon the educational scene of one abstract doctrine of man would, from the Christian point of view, lead to grievous errors, stifle creative human activity, and be based upon a fallacious view of the nature of man himself.

The interdependence of the knowledge of God and the knowledge of man, already noted, leads to a further insight regarding the crisis in higher education. Since the nineteenth century when Nietzsche first elucidated the idea, many intellectuals in the Western world have been proclaiming that "God is dead." The outcome of this death of God in Nietzsche's thinking was the necessity for superman. The situation was like that of a family that has lost its chief and in which the growing son must mature rapidly to fulfill the role of the dead father. Nietzsche's superman found its unexpected fulfillment in the Hitlerian dream of the superrace. Many of the most sensitive members of the intelligentsia who have accepted Nietzsche's claim have not been celebrating the advent of superman but rather mourning the death of man. Since every image of man is really an image of God and every image of God an image of man, the crisis in our society may be seen in terms of the loss of man attendant upon the loss of God.[46]

Christians following the argument thus far should be able to anticipate the obvious relevance of Christology at this very point. For it is the claim of the traditional Christian theology that in Jesus Christ we have an image of man that is also an image of God. This image was not created by man but given to man, given to him in the flesh and not merely an abstract statement.[47] In Jesus Christ, Christian theology maintains, we see true God and true man. It would seem, then, that Christians have a significant contribution to make to a discussion centering around images of man. The Christian community is to embody the life of Christ in the world. The church is not well equipped, however, at the present time, to manifest this embodiment or to engage in the dialogue that flows from it. It is almost as confused about its image of Christ as the world is about its views of man. This confusion is clearly illustrated in contemporary Christian art. How does the church portray Jesus of Nazareth? Is he the lily-handed boy with the permanent walking along with the fleecy sheep, of the magenta-colored Sunday school bulletins? Or is he the Nordic idealist of the various popular paintings of the head of Christ? [48] The church is not sure which, if either.

One of the most pressing tasks of the day is for the church to rethink and articulate its Christology so that it may proclaim and live out in the midst of culture an image of man as seen in Christ. This image will not be the only view of man witnessed to in our society. Other views should also be delineated. The issue between the pluralistic communities of commitment that make up American society is not simply divergent theological or philosophical emphases but contrasting views of human nature.[49] Varying humanist views of man should also be articulated within the university, where encounters and dialogues between these differing views should be encouraged.

This crisis of our age, centering on our images of man, is also reflected in our attitude toward truth. Pilate's question "What is truth?" is still a good one and needs to be answered. All departments within a modern university claim to teach the truth, but are rather befuddled when asked the simple question: "What is the truth that is taught? Is it absolute, or is it relative?" Christians cannot be satisfied with the understanding of truth seen as a sum of facts or a collection of true statements. Rather, truth must be seen in the light of a framework that man does not create but which he brings to the learning situation. That framework is the reality of man. It is the human image and therefore also the divine image. Man is not free to choose his reality. He is not free to choose the truth. The truth determines man, not man the truth. Surely this is the New Testament view of truth. This is the truth that must grasp us. This is the truth that is personal. But this truth must be true not only for us but for others, or communication is impossible. All communication presumes the interpersonal character of truth. Education therefore presumes community or interpersonality. When we share reality we can communicate. The crisis in the university is the breakdown of the interpersonality of reality and therefore of truth.

Herein lies the evil that flows from specialization and the atomization of knowledge. The Oxford medieval historian, Marjorie Reeves, has written: "Our root problem . . . lies in a failure of confidence in the value of knowledge. We do not believe in what we study or teach as really meaningful, and therefore we do not believe in ourselves as teachers. Having nothing, so it seems, worth transmitting, we try to transmit nothing. But this is impossible; we cannot fail to impart some attitude to our pupils and so, in the endeavor to avoid positive preaching, we tend to convey our very scepticism about what we are doing." [50] In the modern university one finds at least three views of reality corresponding to various dominant world views. In science, reality is generally thought of as a world of facts dominated by law. All, including man, is explicable. In historical disciplines, one sees reality viewed as a world of conflicting values, freely chosen, made, and changed by man. In the realm of art and religion, human experience is seen as pointing beyond itself to a hidden transcendent truth revealing itself in symbolic form. Behind each of these views of reality lies a view of man. In the crisis for truth we see the crisis of modern man; we see the indecision about the nature of reality and therefore about man; we become aware of the indecision about truth and how it is achieved.

Will Herberg has made the interesting observation that only two images of man have been dominant in the history of higher education in the Western world.[51] The image of man as rational animal is the dominant one behind the classical university, and the image of man as adaptive animal is the contribution of what Sir Walter Moberly calls the modern "political university." Herberg has noted that it is strange that a Biblical view of man has never formed the basis for a complete educational philosophy.[52]

To spell out in terms of an educational system what a Biblical view of man might mean would appear to be one of the possible challenges today for the church-related college. In such an attempt man would be seen not merely as a rational and adaptive animal, but also as a covenantal animal.[53] Man may be viewed as one who lives by his commitment and by his faith. In this connection it is instructive to remember the place of commitment in the discovery of truth in the Biblical perspective. In the Old Testament the verb "to know" is used as a euphemism for sexual relations. "Adam knew Eve his wife, and she conceived and bore Cain." What this implies is that knowledge takes place within total involvement and commitment and not just by detachment or thoroughgoing objectivity. Perhaps it is not strange that a generation steeped in an understanding of knowledge derived from detached observation should be irresponsible in the application of that knowledge. Such a scientific approach to knowledge could well be balanced with this Biblical conception.

The Biblical view of man as the base for an educational system would modify the view of truth. Truth would not be seen as something passive to be discovered, over which man has control and which he manipulates; truth would be viewed as something active and challenging, something that grasps man and changes him. The Biblical view of man's sin also has important implications for education. In the Biblical perspective man is free, and because he is free he is anxious, and in his anxiety he continually constructs premature securities. These premature securities may dominate the whole of his life, including his intellectual life. Christian faith reminds man of the contingency of his life, world, systems of thought, and ideologies.[54] This means that education from a Biblical perspective must take into account a dialectical process. Other positions are necessary to correct a man's imperfect view of the truth. The Christian should be above all educable because he has no ideology, *Weltanschauung,* or pet theory that for him has become the ultimate. His only ultimate is Jesus Christ and he is not an abstract principle but a person. The advice given by Herbert Butterfield in the last line of his book *Christianity and History,* "Hold to Christ, and for the rest be totally uncommitted,"[55] describes the position of the person who is truly open for encounter, discussion, and learning.

All truth for the Christian occupies the position referred to by John Oldham as "middle axioms."[56] This means that all positions in every field, including that of theology, occupy only a secondary position. They are not themselves the ultimate but are only adequate insofar as they point to the ultimate. Theories and systems thus occupy a middle position between the absolute (Christ himself) and the particular situation or reality under observation or analysis.

Finally it may be noted that from a Biblical perspective man learns within community. Community is the locus for the courage to face the truth about man, and it is also the locus of obedience to God and responsibility for neighbor. The freedom to become a person is found within community and the relationship between community and communication is obvious on every side.

Chapter Six

✠

Problems and Issues in the University

No institution — save perhaps the church — has more problems than the university. It has long been observed by many writers that the university is a microcosm of the world — a little universe having all the problems of the world. One can scarcely mention an issue in our general cultural life that is not reflected to some degree or in some way in the university. And since we live in a problem-filled age we can properly talk about a problem-filled university.

Problems and the university go together for another reason. This is because the university has a vested interest in problems since it may be defined as a problem-solving institution. We must limit ourselves, perforce, to the exploration of a few key problems in higher education, problems that are specially relevant to the church's mission in this field.

The first problem is the role of theory in the modern university. We may well ask about the impact of theories concerning the university on the concrete realities of higher education. What is the relationship between all the books that are being written about what the university ought to be and actual universities? What role does theory play in the life of higher educational institutions? A second issue flows from an anticipated answer to the first question. This is the problem of the pressures that are making the university over into the image of a modern business corporation. The university in our day is in danger of becoming not so much the locus for the pursuit of disinterested truth as a corporation for the production of a number of products. Higher education may cease to fulfill its function as an independent critic of culture and become a supplier of goods and services along with all sorts of other corporations in our society. The third question is, How may the university and church support each other so that each may fulfill its own proper role?

We are dealing with aspects of what has commonly been called "the university question." Many of the problems with which people have been wrestling in the field of higher education in the past few years have been problems raised by Christians within the university. Churchmen in the period immediately after the Second World War became very concerned about the university. Two well-known works from this period typify this interest: Sir Walter Moberly's *The Crisis in the University* and John Coleman's *The Task of the Christian in the University*.[57]

After World War II there was a general feeling that there ought to be a radical reappraisal of the role of the university in Western culture, and Christians were among the first to be sensitive to this issue. Some of the problems raised by Christian writers were perennial and will continue to be debated within the university and outside of it for the foreseeable future. But some of the problems raised then have been so well discussed as to be virtually solved — insofar as anything of a theological or philosophical nature is ever solved. An example is provided by The Hazen Foundation pamphlet by Marjorie Reeves, *Three Questions in Higher Education*, to which we have already made reference. Miss

Reeves asked, "Ought a teacher to indoctrinate a pupil?" This might have been a very good question when it was raised, but it is one today that is no longer regarded as being a lively issue among faculty. It is widely recognized that the teacher should accept the role of his total personality in the teaching process. And certainly no one within the campus ministry would say that a faculty member ought to be indoctrinating students. An answer to that question has been almost universally accepted.

Miss Reeves also asked, "Are academic studies autonomous?" The answer is simply no. Even the so-called pure sciences exist within the context of a greater responsibility. In the last century, John Henry Cardinal Newman observed that if there has to be any justification for a college course, it must be presumed that the good of society is ultimately in consideration. The good of society supposedly undergirds all teaching within a university.

The third question raised was, "Should a Christian university or college be primarily an institution to nurture the young in the faith?" All but the most conservative of the church-related colleges would be uncomfortable if they thought that they existed solely to nurture youth in religion. Thus we have three questions that apparently were lively issues at the end of the war which since have been, to a large degree, resolved.

If we go back to this immediately postwar period, we note that Christians were among the first to suggest the need for university curriculum revision. Sir Richard Livingston, of Corpus Christi College at Oxford, stated in an article published shortly after the war that the individual undergraduate courses were good but that undergraduate education has never been thought out as a whole. Since that time an increasing amount of attention has been given to curriculum revision. There is general awareness today of the need for educational goals that will integrate study and for curricula that will take this into account. Curriculum revision is at least being considered in many institutions these days, so that most educators are aware of the problems noted in an address in 1946 by Walter Lippmann to the American Association for the Advancement of Science when he observed, "We have established a system of education in which we insist that everyone should be educated, yet there is nothing in particular that an educated man must know."

Christians also have alerted many within the university to the problem of academic objectivity. Is it possible to teach a course with complete detachment or objectivity? In the past fifteen years, the issue of presuppositions has been much discussed, and we have come to a fairly general recognition that there are presuppositions behind every discipline. We have recovered the idea that a professor professes — that he does have some commitments and that these commitments influence his view of man, the subject matter he teaches, or the manner in which he teaches it. But despite the fact that Christians raised questions such as those we have just noted, some of which have been solved, there are today still many unresolved issues in the university. A recent remark by Robert M. Hutchins has reminded us of the continued urgency of basic problems within the life of the university. Dr. Hutchins stated: "I believe that the purpose of the university is to be a center of independent criticism, but I do not know of any university that fulfills this role at the present time in the United States. I would say, therefore, in my opinion, there is not a true university in the United States today." [58] This is a rather strong indictment of American education. The comment is related to the first of the issues we are to discuss — the role of the theory of the university in actual modern higher education.

Ideas and theories about higher education are important to the modern university, but they do not determine its nature. The theory of the university is, if I may use the term, superstructural. It is not necessary to be a Marxist to accept this. There is a basis for this in incarnational theology. W. H. Auden has observed that the words of a dead man are modified in the guts of the living. We might say that the words of educators are modified by the realities of university existence. Writers such as Dr. Hutchins are reminding us today of the ancient claim that the university exists for the pursuit and transmission of disinterested truth. The university is ideally to be a center of independent critique for all of man's endeavors. A university is not just a trade school teaching vocational techniques. Neither should it be a high school that exists merely to transmit the values of the culture in which it exists. The university is, theoretically, a " universal " institution. It can never afford to be provincial in its outlook. Faculty and students are called to be a part of a universal company of scholars. All this is being said by many voices in our day, and yet, in practice, not much of this is being actualized. Ideas that we have inherited from the classical past are being restated on every side, but apparently without effect. Just within the last few years Newman's *Idea of a University* has been reissued, and in 1959 an English translation of Karl Jaspers' book, *The Idea of the University,* appeared.[59] It is instructive to observe the reasons given for Jaspers' writing of this book. They are to be found in the preface by Karl Deutsch which provides us with the background for this restatement of time-honored ideals. Deutsch says: " It was the memory of the thousands of students who had forsaken the books of Kant for the loudspeakers of Goebbels and the jack boots of the elite guard; the professors who had eagerly believed the nationalistic and racial propaganda, forsaking their standards of critical thinking; and those other professors who, while not believing the doctrines of the Third Reich, yet found it prudent to pretend belief, and not deceived, yet aided the deceivers."[60] Jaspers' restatement of the ancient ideals of the university was prompted by the memory of the way in which these ideals had been bypassed and subverted within what was the best educated country in Western Europe.

But despite this restatement of the ideals, the facts of the modern university are, as Dr. Hutchins noted, in many ways disturbingly remote from these standards. The university that is conscious of such obvious tyranny as that represented by the Nazis, and is suspicious of the heteronomous control that the church once represented in Western culture, is still extremely naïve about new forms of domination. One primary danger of our time is that the university may abdicate its critical function in the culture almost completely. If this happened, the conscience of society might cease to fulfill one of its principal tasks, and become merely a tool in the national defense. A major problem therefore centers around this question, Will the university in the United States today sell itself as an adjunct to the national defense? If it does, then it has abdicated two roles of the ancient university: the critical role and its part in the universal company of scholars. William Lee Miller comments on this latter danger in a pamphlet issued by the Woodrow Wilson Foundation, *Education and Some American Temptations*. Miller writes: May one not say that education serves the nation best when it is not too strictly concerned to be 'in the nation's service.' There must be something beyond the nation that it serves, or something worthwhile without regard to services rendered, in order even for education to have the quality that the nation needs! "

In our day, government, big business, and special interest groups may by their grants and influence pervert the true function of the university. The university does not really serve the needs of our age when it is bent on serving them uncritically.

Jaspers' conception of the university also holds that individual initiative and responsibility must be increased within the university and that higher standards of academic work must continually be sought. Jaspers states that "the very nature of the university demands . . . that the individual exercise his own choices throughout his entire course of study at the acknowledged risk of ending up with nothing. Hence, our most serious and ultimately insoluble problem is how to create an intellectual and institutional climate at the university favorable to such independence."[61] One of the problems for the faculty is how to tear down the comfortable supports of the student so that he can really become free and independent in making his choices. This is an interesting theory; but in practice we find a tendency toward uniformity and mediocrity in college programs. In part this is a penalty of mass education, the result of a cafeteria view of the university. One campus in the Midwest distributes matchbooks that have on the cover the caption, "Learn a better living." The implication is, of course, that the university is primarily a trade-school institution. What the student is told is that education is not pursuit of truth, not involvement of the person in the creative frontiers of human knowledge; rather, it is acquiring techniques that are marketable.

Uniformity in education is aided and abetted by forces within the university itself. Ingrown faculties are one of the major problems here. Faculties tend to get replacements from other "approved" institutions, which become so approved because they represent the prevailing opinion of the faculty already employed. Thus faculties have a tendency to become introverted, to become inbred.[62]

Some deans of students' offices work tirelessly against Jaspers' thesis. They are primarily organized to keep students in college who ought to be gotten out of college. The premise of their effort is that to keep students in college is financially desirable, since they represent an investment that would otherwise be lost. Thus it frequently occurs that there is tension in the university between the dean of students' office and the faculty, the former concerned about retaining a substandard student, and the faculty feeling that the student ought to do some very good work and if not he ought to get out.

Many factors are at work in our society that also mitigate against the classical ideals that are held up for the university. These factors dull the critical function of the university, challenge its aristocratic principles, and tend to transfer it into purely an urbane vocational ground for government and big business. This is why one of the great issues of higher education is what we have referred to in our second question dealing with the university as a corporation.

The dominant pattern for American higher education is not so much the Western intellectual heritage of the university as the industrial technical corporation — the chief institution of our economic society. One can see this in the tremendous increase in the power of the university administrators. No longer are university administrators what they originally were — bureaucrats serving the faculty, office boys for the teaching staff who are the real heart of the university. Deans and administrators have become management employing the faculty who are now the workers, and the students, of course, are the customers. We are living in a time of the proletarianization of the faculty who tend to become wage earners employed by the university. It is not strange, therefore, that evaluation of faculty suddenly becomes based upon criteria of output. You publish or you perish! The amount that is published and the journal in which it is published become the criteria on which promotion is to be based. So the university administration begins to parallel the functions of management in a large corporation. The mentality of the corporation is also reflected in the cost-price squeeze that lies behind some of the arguments heard for such new academic schemes as the trimester system. It has been advocated that universities ought to adopt the trimester plan because of " the increased number of bodies served "!

The corporation ethos is furthered also through the control of boards of trustees and the pressure of alumni groups who are primarily business-oriented. The grounds upon which such people evaluate the institution tend to be imported from the field of production, sales, and service. There is a tremendous challenge in our day to educate boards of trustees to the proper function of such groups in higher education.

Also to be reckoned with is that " at large " board of trustees, the alumni. They tend to have the same role in the university that satisfied customers do in the business world. That is to say, they influence policy. The alumni are either satisfied or unsatisfied. University administrators want alumni to be satisfied, and generally they find them satisfied not so much by solid academic improvements as by flashy programs and athletic successes. This also is true of fraternity and sorority alumni. They exercise an influence on the policies of their sororities and fraternities and through them student life as a whole.

Dr. Hans Hofmann, of Harvard, has commented on how faculty attitudes have been subtly influenced by this corporation mentality. The educator who is engaged in a nonscientific or nontechnical field does not produce anything that is very tangible in our society. You can't see the results of his work. And yet a corporation-oriented society expects the results of activity to be capable of measurement. The educator in the field of humanities is made to feel that he is not understood or properly valued because he doesn't produce in this tangible fashion. The result may be either a conscious or unconscious feeling of inferiority that induces a further retreat into specialization in an age that understands specialization, or a tendency to sell oneself to the highest bidder and become highly opportunistic in the educational enterprise.

In short, it may be feared that the image of the large corporation is more important than the historic models for the American university today. Those persons who guide the destiny of these institutions have a great sensitivity to what is known as the "P.R. image," a judicious combination of high ideals, hard facts, and whatever the public expectation may be.

Lest churchmen begin to feel a bit smug at this point, it is necessary to note that the only institution that reflects even more of the corporation image in our society is the church. Of course, the university and the church are always going to reflect their society to some degree. The question at the moment is whether the prevailing images further or deter these institutions in their essential tasks. Well might it be asked what the university and church may do to serve each other in the light of this mutual problem.

Both the university and the church are called to fulfill what may be called the role of servant-critic in our society. One reason for the historic tension between the university and the church is that they are so close to each other in the roles which they are called to fulfill. Both institutions know, when they are reflecting their best traditions, that the only good critic is one who serves and the only one who really serves the society is one who has the courage to criticize it.

But each institution, university and church, has a different prevailing temptation. It is the temptation of the church in our day to be overly critical. Especially is this true when the church is conscious of the fact that it no longer directly shapes the major institutions of our society. When one is not responsible, one falls very easily into a critical role. The church frequently criticizes the university without serving it. Frequently one finds groups of pastors in college town churches who are negative about the universities around them but have spent little time in discussion among responsible groups in their own churches about the needs and problems of higher education.

The university in our time tends to be overly servile. It wants to be the almost uncritical servant of society. It is happy to sell itself to big business or to big government or to anyone who will finance its expensive undertakings without being too critical about what this service might mean. The university wants to be a servant in our society, but it thinks the best way to serve is by not being too critical. The university should remind the church of the necessity of service within the life of society, and the church ought to remind the university of the role that it characteristically has fulfilled as critic of society — including the church. One way in which the university might be encouraged to reestablish its critical function is if the church were to invite, accept, and utilize whatever critiques may be forthcoming of the church by the university.

Church and university need the mutual support that comes from continual dialogue between them. The church needs the university with its synoptic criticism of society and its historical perspective to redeem the church from its smugness and parochialness of concern. And the university needs the illumination of faith regarding the worthwhileness of its goals to save it from becoming captive to alien forces that would destroy its essential function.

Sometimes the university does not want to be saved. It prefers the plush life of Government contracts to the rather rarefied atmosphere of being a center of independent critique. And the church frequently will not support such an independent university. It wants to keep the university under tight control. The structures of the church's institutional forms frequently do not permit the church to respond to the university's needs.

We have noted but three basic problems within the life of the university — problems with which churchmen ought to be concerned and about which the church could do something. It is a profound Protestant belief that Biblical faith still has the power to transform not only men but institutions. It is fascinating to read in the first book of the Bible how the tree of knowledge is first presented as a threat to man. Genesis would seem to tell us that when man grasps knowledge for his own purposes, when man uses this knowledge in a way in which he is not responsible either to God or to his neighbor, then this knowledge becomes the source of man's damnation. But at the other end of the Bible in the book of The Revelation, there is the tree of knowledge again, but here its leaves are used for the healing of the nations. This would seem to tell us that knowledge is always two-edged — full of threat as well as promise — but that knowledge for redeemed man has a healing quality that is absolutely essential. We seem to be living somewhere in between the threat of Genesis and the eschatological perspective of The Revelation. Will the tree of knowledge in our day be for the healing of the nations or will it lead to the further damnation of man? The church cannot but be sacrificially involved in the whole life of the university while that issue is still in doubt.

Chapter Seven

✠

The Role of Community in Education

THERE IS A TRADITION in our Western culture that learning is somehow closely related to community. The university is thought of as an academic *community* because the process of knowing in some way takes place in interpersonal relations. The writings of Martin Buber have greatly contributed to the recapturing in our day of this ancient understanding. We are coming again to appreciate the value of dialogue in education. The goal in this view of education is not to project the teacher on the student so as to make the student conform to some general model, nor to draw out the student in a situation in which the teacher never reveals his true position but merely acts as a catalyst for the student's thinking, but the goal is a true encounter between student and teacher. Marjorie Reeves has written: "In the New Testament, God's Truth is given to men, not in a series of intellectual propositions, but in the One Person who perfectly embodies the divine Being. God *meets* men in Jesus Christ; reality is apprehended in and through relationships. Surely in this dimly-understood revelation of God's plan, we must find a basis for our own conception of education. . . . It is difficult to avoid the conclusion that, if God has so ordained human growth, we must accept its consequences, accept, that is to say, our own human personalities as God-given instruments of education, accept unshrinkingly the responsibility for influencing our pupils, accept the belief that to remain disengaged is to evade our real task as teachers." [63] What Miss Reeves insists upon is that it be recognized that knowledge of the truth requires interpersonal relationships — requires, that is to say, community — and is based upon a degree of involvement and personal commitment. Even scientific knowledge takes place within a community and presumes commonly accepted canons of evidence drawn up by that community. It is within this dialogic view of education that response may become responsibility. Responsible knowledge, therefore, is related to a committed community.

We are indebted not only to Martin Buber but also to Paul Tillich for recalling something that has deep roots in Western culture. Tillich has shown the relationship between anxiety and courage in the quest for truth.[64] What Tillich emphasizes can be seen most clearly when it is seen against the background of an older, generally accepted educational theory. In this older theory education consists merely in the transmission of valueless facts from the pages of books or minds of professors into the minds of the students. The only factors really involved are the articulateness of the professor, the clarity of the writing, or the I.Q. of the student. This view of education sees it as a rather simple process.

But we are realizing anew that education is a far more complex affair. In the university the learning experience normally involves anxiety on the part of students and requires a degree of personal courage in order that truth may be accepted. The following factors must be taken into account in any attempt to understand higher education. The student who has reached college age has already developed a certain world view or general way of viewing reality, including himself. This world view cannot but be inadequate because of the limited experience of the individual who comes out of a single family experience and one particular culture. What happens in university education is that a student, with this limited background, is suddenly exposed to the accumulated knowledge of mankind. This accumulated knowledge of mankind threatens the world view already accepted; indeed, most students' world views require much readjustment, if not complete reconstruction. A student, however, is not detached from his world view. It is his characteristic way of approaching and understanding reality. Indeed, it is closely identified with his understanding of himself. Therefore, anything that threatens the world view threatens the student. Higher education cannot help producing anxiety in the mind of the student, because the truth it presents requires a restructuring of the self.

Of course, the simplest way to deal with this type of threatening knowledge is not to listen to it. Young people in our society have learned the technique of selective listening. It is absolutely essential, in a culture in which one is barraged with varying advertising attempts to gain one's attention, to learn to listen selectively. This process, so essential for sanity, is misapplied when the student refuses to listen to that which challenges his own world view. A disturbing percentage of students do exactly that, learning only enough facts to pass the required examinations but never seriously grappling with the truth which the university wishes to communicate. The study *Changing Values in College,* by Phillip E. Jacob,[65] indicates how little the experience of higher education, in its formal academic aspects, affects the student's value patterns. This study indicates that it is the personal contacts and relationships with faculty beyond the classroom that have an impact on changing student values. This would suggest that community relationships or interpersonal relationships are necessary before a person can overcome the anxiety raised by the educational experience.

One might say, then, that anxiety is present in any community engaged in the exploration of truth. And the only way in which this anxiety may be lived with is when the individual finds himself openly accepted in such a community. Education is the introduction of a person into a community of scholars which has the courage to face threatening truth. Here the function of the teacher is to break down the student's anxiety and help him have the courage to grow into a larger world.[66]

What we are returning to is a classical view of education as *sapientia* and not just as *scientia*. The aim of classical education was to grasp the total situation in terms of the total environment. This involves an increase in anxiety that can only be allayed through the acquisition of courage. Hence Plato's remark that only the courageous man can know the truth.

The relevance of an understanding of community as the context within which education may take place to the problems of a recovery of a sense of values in society is quite obvious. Certainly one aspect of the Christian contribution toward the solution of the university question may be in its witness to the interpersonality or essentially communal nature of truth.

There would seem to be a tremendous opportunity here for the church-related college to provide such a committed community where education may proceed from a clearly stated set of Christian presuppositions. In the church-related college an open fellowship of Christians, regularly renewed in common worship, may be the context for individual freedom and growth. Such a community must, however, be aware of the dangers of theologies becoming ideologies. We must recall that other positions are necessary to prove a corrective to the limited truth of our own position and that a true dialectic is the basis of all advance in human thinking.

Herein would also lie a tremendous opportunity for campus Christian fellowships in the large state and private universities. Within these communities of learning there exist communities of faith where new truth may be accepted with courage and where the environment for the exploration of threatening truth could be provided. In these centers the Christian faith may be presented as an option, and an encounter may take place between Christian faith and human wisdom to the benefit of both.[67] Christian faith may establish the worthwhileness of academic pursuits based upon man's God-given role as having dominion over creation.[68] Just because the Christian community is not dependent upon an ideology but upon a person, it should be free from the intransigence of established theories, be open to new truth on every side, and indeed view all human formularies and truths as merely "middle axioms."

What has been said about the potential role of the church-related college and the campus Christian community unfortunately lies in the field of theory. This is because there has been a general failure to establish significant community on a Christian basis within the church-related college or on the campuses of the state and private universities. There is today little sense of community within the church, its institutions, or in the world at large. However, there is a tremendous interest and concern for community in our whole culture. One can see this from communal fads like square dance groups all the way to the concern for the United Nations. This is due to a general awareness of the breakdown of human community in our culture. It is generally true that where there is a strong sense of something there may be little discussion of it.[69]

The great increase in various forms of conformity in our culture is an indication of the lack of true community. This is based upon an error that involves an understandable but regrettable confusion between conformity and community. The observations of a Greek Orthodox in attending Protestant worship and a Protestant attending Greek Orthodox worship is illustrative of this point. The Protestant found the Orthodox service extremely bewildering because people did not seem to be doing things together. They got up, wandered about, stood around, entered, and left, without any seeming pattern of behavior. The Greek Orthodox observed that Protestant worship was something like a military drill in which everyone did everything together. The Orthodox commented that the freedom of the individual in Orthodox worship may be indicative of a very strong sense of community among the Orthodox. No one felt threatened by the individuality of the worship of his fellows, whereas the Protestant was dependent upon the conformity of others in order to have a sense of communal worship. Here we have a witness to the way in which true community can liberate the individual, whereas conformity can be easily confused with community.

It is extremely important that we come to some understanding of the meaning of community. For this study it is particularly significant to note what some contemporary theologians say about the nature of human community. Clyde Holbrook in his book *Faith and Community* has brought together some significant definitions from a variety of theologians.[70]

R. L. Calhoun defines community as " a corporate group in which diversity, unity, freedom, and discipline are subtly related, all contributing to the deep unity of life.[71] Daniel Day Williams sees the role of community in the development of the *person* when he notes that community is " the order in which the members of society are so related that the freedom, uniqueness, and power of each serves the freedom, uniqueness, and growth of all the other members." [72] It is Nels Ferré whose definition stresses the divine ground of all community: " By community we mean a psychic social and spiritual reality rooted in God's activity in history. . . . Such community becomes more or less concrete in history." [73] Rudolf Bultmann claims that community must involve personal interrelatedness. He states that there are four forms of community but that only the last two constitute full community. First there is the community developed by nature, and, secondly, the community developed by history; then there is the community founded on the intellectual world of art and science (which might be referred to as the community founded by the university), and, lastly, the community founded by religion. The distinction between the community developed by nature and one developed by history will be very important for consideration later on. Emil Brunner notes that only man has community, for it involves the necessity of free decision. It is also the necessary context for love.[74] In reading Holbrook's analysis, one notes two divergent tendencies among these theological definitions of community. One is to root it in the human personality, as with Calhoun, Williams, and Brunner. The other is to root it in God's action, as with Nels Ferré. Holbrook himself tries to take a stance that will provide room for both positions by basing community upon God's act, not in redemption as with Ferré, but in God's act in creation. Holbrook writes, " We begin by accepting not the nature of personality as determinative of community but the unity which God gives in his creation of this world as one world, and the pressure to unity which is exhibited in its relevant forms at every level of His world." [75]

From Holbrook's analysis of the issue we may choose three significant insights that assist us in a theological understanding of the nature of community. First of all, there is the purpose of God as manifested in creation; that is, the structures of creation seem to move toward the development of a community of interrelatedness in love. The second ground of community is in the unique personal nature of man. For it is within community that man develops the uniqueness of his creative self because community provides both freedom and discipline for the development of the self. And thirdly, there is an indication of specific historic events that have been the occasion of binding men together within communities. Certainly there are many other sociological, geographical, economic, and political factors that might be considered in the formation of specific communities. A recognition of these factors must be presumed, but they are not the essential ingredients of the communities of faith or learning, for these communities have in fact developed despite supposed barriers raised by some of these factors. Common geography, common language, common economic interests, all may be factors within the development of human community, but they are not determinative.

There is a major rationalist error with respect to community to which we are particularly subject due to our professional bias as students and teachers and to the history of Western liberal political thought. This is the " social contract " theory of community. It is derived, of course, from the contribution of such philosophers and political theorists as Hobbes, Rousseau, and Locke. Hobbes made an erroneous presumption of a " state of nature " in which all men were at war with all others before the development of the community, which was a rational answer to the problem of individual safety. Rousseau and Locke also saw the political community as the application of man's mind to social problems with an increasingly rational control over more primitive social forms and structures. We are indebted to Reinhold Niebuhr for exposing the tendency among social contract theorists to overstress the rational rather than the organic basis of community. Niebuhr reminds us that "every human community is both organism and artifact. It is an organism insofar as it is integrated by loyalties, forms of cohesion, and hierarchies of authority which have grown unconsciously with a minimum of conscious contrivance. . . . The community and its authorities are artifacts insofar as the form of cohesion and the integration of the community have been consciously contrived." [76] Niebuhr reminds us that government presupposes community but cannot create it. We might say, with respect to the Christian community, that theology and church polity presuppose the Christian community but do not and cannot create it. Reformed Christians are particularly liable to the rationalist error because their branch of Christianity has found the heart of its life in theology. The only other group of Christians more liable to this rationalist temptation are those who find the center of their church life in organization. Both the theologically and organizationally oriented are in quite different positions from those who find their roots in liturgy.[77]

It is necessary to guard against both the romanticist error which sees community in a wholly organic sense without the role of the reason being recognized, and the rationalist error in not recognizing the organic base of community. The proper place of the organic and the rational is a necessary part of understanding human community.

The essential ingredient in all human community beyond

merely the biological level is shared experience. When a group of men and women share a significant experience together, they learn who they are both individually and collectively from that experience and are bound together in community. This understanding of true community as finding its basis in common experience takes into account the factors of the proper relationship between the organic and the rational, the role of freedom and decision, and the understanding of the dependence of the personal upon the interpersonal.

There are two broad types of shared experience. First there is shared empirical experience which is the root of human science. Here conditions are controlled; the experience is repeatable, moving in either direction; and it is universally valid. The Greek poet and philosopher Empedocles in the fifth century B.C. recorded a simple experiment to show that air is a material substance. If one inverts a glass beaker in a tub of water, it is found that the water within the beaker only rises to a certain point. Something must be keeping the water from rising completely within the beaker. This something is air, and thus air is a substance. Such shared empirical experience is inductive in nature and is the basis of all of man's scientific endeavors. The second broad type of shared experience is shared historical experience. Such experience is unrepeatable, moves in only one direction, and has no controlled conditions. By nature it is deductive. Some semanticists have been concerned about the possibility of establishing community among men solely on the basis of shared empirical experiences and luring men away from community based upon deductive experiences.[78] The argument is that community based upon such scientific experiences provides a base for relationships without limits, since empirical experience is universally valid. The argument says that community has unfortunately been based on master symbols — that is, deductively. For example, a Muslim meets a stranger and says, " Great is Allah." If the stranger acknowledges the master symbol and replies, " Allah is great," then community is established. But if the stranger replies, " Jesus is my personal Savior," then what? Obviously, the argument runs, the empirical experience is to be valued over the master-symbol experience. What Hayakawa and other semanticists overlook in their analysis is that all great faiths that provide master symbols as the basis for community, and therefore for communication, also presume universality and on exactly the same basis as the scientific approach. That is, they assume that a shared experience of Allah or Jesus may provide the basis for welding people together within a community. The error the semanticists noted here is the same error that Niebuhr has already noted with respect to the social contract theorists. Both the semanticists and the social contract theorists forget the organic base of community in stressing the role of man's reason in contriving community. They fail to recognize the primacy of certain decisive historic events or experiences in the bringing of people together and establishing human community.

For a community to be truly human, it must be established on the level of history and not merely on the level of nature. This points to another problem with the semanticists' proposition. Shared empirical experience can provide community only on the level of nature, not on the level of history. Herein lies man's grandeur and his misery. For, as Reinhold Niebuhr might say, this means that man achieves the level of community which transcends the natural, but which also, because of his freedom, frequently falls below the level of the natural community of animal life.[79]

Judaism and Christianity are historical religions, not merely in the sense that they are religions with long historic experience within the world, but because the existence of these religious communities is seen as being dependent upon specific historic events in which God has revealed himself. It was the shared *historical* experience of the tribes that made Israel a theocracy rather than the participation in the nature cults of the Canaanite religions. Israel owed its existence to specific historic events: the call of Abraham, the slavery in Egypt, the crossing of the Red Sea, the wandering in the desert, the establishment of the Promised Land, the Babylonic captivity, the restoration of Jerusalem. For the Christian, the community of faith is dependent upon the life, death, and resurrection of Jesus Christ.

The master symbol, which has grown out of a significant historic experience shared by a community, is both organic and rational in nature. For their existence such communities depend upon the role of memory and symbol, which provide opportunity to share in the historical experience of the past, identity in the present, and the means by which the community projects its self-understanding into the future.

The master symbols of Judaism and Christianity center around historic experiences in which the power of God is seen overcoming what appear to be certain human failures or defeats. The crossing of the Red Sea and the resurrection of Christ both point to a God who is capable of turning defeat into victory. Such a God is radically free, and the communities created by him are also free to face the realities of human sin, tragedy, and defeat without cynicism and despair. They may look to the future with hope.

What is peculiar to these communities of faith is important to an understanding of the relationship between them and the community of learning. We must therefore attempt to delineate the nature of the community of faith.

Chapter Eight

✠

Community and Faith

In the last chapter, we noted the role of specific historic events in providing the shared experience that became the basis of the Jewish and the Christian religious communities. This shared historical experience provided master symbols that are both organic and contrived, providing a place for the rational but also establishing the primacy of the organic in the communities of faith. In this religious tradition, faith is an encounter or meeting rather than a rational speculation about probabilities. In analyzing the phenomenon of community, it is necessary to explore another facet of the relationship between the rational and the organic as these are blended together in the nature of religious community.

The theory that lies behind this analysis is what may be called the " status and contract " theory of the development of Western culture. It is a product of my thinking begun by certain conversations with Prof. Vigo A. Demant, of Christ Church College, Oxford. Professor Demant claimed that this insight was a product of his pondering the Biblical record in relation to his own background as a professional sociologist.[80] The value of Demant's theory for our purpose lies in the way in which it helps us to understand the relationship between the rational and organic in community and the manner in which it grew out of an understanding of the experience of the people of God.

Very generally, this theory says that man emerges into history living in communities governed by *status* relationships, but that the development of culture has seen the gradual replacement of these status relationships by *contractual* ones. Man, however, cannot be adjusted to a completely contractual society and seeks to find new status relationships on higher levels, in which alone he can rest and find security, and from which he can move out and be creative.

It is important to understand the meaning of the terms " status " and " contract." The term " status " is used *not* in the sense of Vance Packard's use of the word in *The Status Seekers*. " Status " is used to describe, rather, an organic relationship. This relationship is not contrived but is conferred. It is conferred either naturally, as in the biological status relationships of the human family, or historically, as in the experience of the Jewish tribes coming out of Egypt and forming a nation in Canaan. The *status* being referred to here is conferred status rather than acquired status. The primitive status relationships of the clan placed little emphasis on ethics or the individual. The basic relationship that bound the individual was organic, conferred upon him from outside of himself and not dependent upon his conduct. It is symptomatic of our time that there is less difficulty in understanding what is meant by a contract relationship. This is because we live in a highly contractual society. A contractual relationship is one based upon mutual agreement. It is primarily a rational relationship. In contractual relationships ethics become important, as the relationship between individuals is wholly dependent upon the conduct of those contracting the relationship. Contractual relationships thus tend to emphasize the individual because his performance becomes determinative for the continuation of the relationship. But it is important to note that the emphasis is upon the performance of the individual and not upon the *individual* qua individual, so that more impersonal qualities and factors enter into consideration.

The history of Western man has been characterized by the replacement of the primitive status relationships by more and more contractual relationships and, as we shall note shortly, the frantic attempt to construct new status communities or to revive old ones. This process was tremendously accelerated in the nineteenth century with the emergence of an industrial society, and it has proceeded with increasing speed ever since. The old land-based rural community was destroyed to provide a free labor pool for the emerging capitalism. The rise of an urban society increased contract relationships of all kinds at the expense of the older organic status relationships. We can see the process of the disintegration of the organic type of community and the increase in contractual basis of human relationship proceeding in our own day. The supermarket has virtually replaced the family grocer. The family grocer, however, frequently felt a responsibility for feeding families who were temporarily without means of support, sometimes without any assurance that repayment would ever be made. The supermarket dispenses a greater variety of products more cheaply than the family grocer, but the supermarket is supremely indifferent to the human problems of its customers. In the medical field, the specialist has replaced the old family doctor who was highly respected though not generally the most wealthy member of his community. The general practitioner felt a responsibility for the health of all his neighbors, many of whom he brought into the world, and was frequently repaid in kind with bushels of potatoes, eggs, etc. The fact that the medical profession today is placing an increased emphasis upon treatment of the *whole* patient, rather than on " cases " or " diseases," is an indication of the awareness of an eroding away of values more characteristic of an earlier type of community.

The problem of a virtually complete contractual community is that it eventuates in a society without a base, without roots, which not only disintegrates community life but disintegrates the individual as well. The problem of juvenile delinquency is a good example of a by-product of a contractual society. The anonymity of the urban community, as over against the structures of the previous rural organic community, provides the context in which delinquency may develop. There is a general disappearance of those older status structures of life by which young people in the past learned who they were and how they developed. Another example may be seen in the contemporary breakdown of the understanding of marriage, with the almost exclusive modern emphasis on the contractual side of this relationship. Historically marriage is both a status and a contract relationship, but the contract was based upon the status conferred in the marriage. Now marriage is looked upon as the amalgamation of two companies which may be dissolved if the relationship fails to be mutually beneficial.

There is a modern myth afoot that tends to emphasize a contractual view of man. That is the view of the unlimited adaptability of the human species. It is true that man may adjust himself to widely differing sets of conditions, but not to every condition. He can live at temperatures ranging from far below zero to hundreds of degrees, but not at absolute zero or at millions of degrees.

Status groups are necessary for human life, and where

they do not exist, man seeks to create them. The social contract theory of community, as was mentioned earlier, operates on the fallacy that it is possible to create community based exclusively upon contract. The fact is, however, that true community is always organic as well as rational. It has a " given " element about it and yet it is contrived. The creation of community involves, therefore, not only agreement to sets of conditions or contracts but shared experiences and symbols. Hence the importance of symbols and of initiations in clubs, lodges, fraternities, sororities, etc.[81] The subconscious longing for status groups may be seen in the rash of festival queens who reign periodically over our contractual society, and in the tremendous American interest in the British monarchy. It is interesting that a contractual republican form of government should breed a strong interest in the older monarchial status type of governmental relationship. But modern man's search and demand for status groups is not as innocent as festival queens or the supposed romance of the Middle Ages. Most of contemporary history may be seen as a frantic and demonic search for status or organic community. The drive toward various forms of collectivism, whether Nazi or Communist, is based upon a class membership of an organic kind, whether this be membership in the Aryan race or in the proletariat. Indeed, the rise of nationalism, which interestingly enough parallels the growth of an industrial or contractual society, may be seen as the emphasis upon a status relationship being increased due to the dwindling of other status relationships of a more local variety. Some analysts have been puzzled that the rise of capitalism has been accompanied by the rise of nationalism, although the two are in conflict. This phenomenon can be, at least in part, explained by the status-contract analysis. The development of capitalism with its contractual emphasis must be accompanied by a growing compensation in some other area — in this case that of national status relationships.

Both Paul Tillich and Reinhold Niebuhr have commented on the flight of modern man from Enlightenment rationalism to modern organic collectives of one sort or another. Tillich notes: "The rush toward standardization and collectivization within modern society is an indirect quest for a spiritual center. . . . The reaction against empty individualism leads to a demonic collectivism."[82] And Niebuhr notes: "The bourgeois individual who emerges from the social cohesions, restraints, and inertias of medievalism and imagines himself master of nature and history, perishes ingloriously in the fateful historical necessities and the frantically constructed tribal solidarities of the age of decay. The lower middle classes fashion this solidarity out of corrupted forms of romanticism [Fascism]; and the proletariat class conceives a philosophy of history which supplants the bourgeois sense of historical mastery with a sense of submission to historical destiny [Communism]."[83]

The demonic nature of the modern collective consists in its ruthless subordination of the individual to the collective, the loss of personal freedom, responsibility, and creativity. This collectivism confuses conformity with community, and what is more, the community created is parasitical upon whatever basic community preceded it. For example, Nazi Germany attempted to revive the already extant Nordic myths, and it is obvious in the present day that Russian Communism is dependent upon the Russian nationalism that existed long before it.

What is more disturbing about the rise of the new demonic status groups is the destructively competitive nature of the solidarity achieved by them. That is, they require that there be those outside of the new status group in order that that status group might exist. This type of community identifies itself by exclusion. We can see this most obviously in the revival of the primitive instincts in modern nationalism. The question naturally arises as to whether a status community might exist which is essentially noncompetitive — that is, which does not require that there be some men not in the community for the community to have a sense of identity and yet which would transcend and give meaning to the many natural communities, including the national communities, which will continue to exist. This is the question asked by Arnold Toynbee in his quest for a new religion. Toynbee says that only a religion can provide the type of community man needs, and of such religion he says that it must possess "an idea of human fraternity that will overcome the clash of cultures . . . and . . . these new societies, which are open to all human beings, with no discrimination between cultures, classes, or sexes, also [must] bring their human members into a saving fellowship with a superhuman being."[84] Despite Toynbee's bypassing of Judaism and Christianity because of their so-called exclusivism, it may be claimed that the type of community which Christianity ideally envisions is one that does not require that there be those outside of it in order for it to be itself. It is indeed instructive to look at Judaism and Christianity from the perspective of this status-contract analysis.

It was noted before that this analysis in the thinking of V. A. Demant grew out of his reading of the Biblical history. Demant noted that Israel was a people brought into existence by a tribal deity. It was a nation based upon a status relationship of an organic kind. Yahweh was the God of the Israelite community without much regard, initially, for the individual members of the community. There was little stress on morality in early Judaism, little sense of the worth of the individual, and, interestingly enough, no doctrine of personal survival after death. As the Old Testament developed, this status relationship with God was supplemented by a contract relationship. This was the conception of the covenant between God and his chosen people. If Israel did certain things, God would fulfill his part of the contract, give them the Promised Land, and protect them. The law developed and ethical monotheism emerged. The individual began to grow in importance, and a doctrine of the resurrection of the dead appeared. The extensive development of legalism within Judaism tended to obscure the basic status relationship upon which Israel was founded. The prophets protested two opposite traits in Israel: on the one hand, the self-confident attitude that so stressed the organic base of their community as to blunt the moral imperatives of faith, and, on the other hand, the rigorous zeal that overemphasized the performance of the Law and slighted the gracious act of God which made Israel a nation and was the basis of the giving of the law.

It became increasingly obvious that the first contract or covenant was unsatisfactory, first of all because it was continually violated on Israel's side by sin, and also because the elaboration of the contract in Pharisaic legalism hid the fact that it was based upon a graciously conferred status relationship. It also became clear that the contract proved too restrictive, for it engendered a nationalism that hindered rather than furthered the purpose for which Israel was called, that through Israel all the nations of mankind might be blessed.

Christianity fulfilled and surpassed Judaism in that it replaced the old contract or covenant with a new contract, covenant, or testament, which was in fact more than another contract. It was, rather, a new status relationship. The gospel declared that man had been brought into a new relationship with God, a status relationship, as adopted sons in Jesus Christ. The language of the New Testament is the language not of contract but of status. It speaks of the Kingdom of God, of men being made joint heirs with Christ. Its chief sacrament is a family meal. The whole mood of the New Testament message may be summarized in the Fourth Gospel's statement in which Jesus says to the disciples, "No longer do I call you servants . . . ; but I have called you friends." Here we have spelled out clearly the transition from a contractual to a status relationship. As L. S. Thornton, a close friend of V. A. Demant's, has written: "Thus filial privileges were submerged under a contractual status no better than that of slaves; for the contract can never be fulfilled. To deal with this frustration of his covenant God sent forth his Son into this world to become man under the conditions of the Jewish Law, in order to redeem those who were under its servitude and restore them to the status of sons." [85]

But this new status relationship was not a denial of the covenant or of the law, nor merely a return to a primitive organic community. It did not deny the law or the place of ethics or the value of the individual, but rather set them in their proper perspective. Christian ethics was no longer "in order to" win God's favor; it rather flowed from gratefulness "because of" what God had done in adopting man in Jesus Christ. It became the human response to God's gracious act of calling him to sonship in Jesus Christ. The root of the new status community, the New Israel, the church, was the shared experience of justification by faith. This shared experience was made possible by God's action in the life, death, and resurrection of Jesus Christ.

Faith then becomes a response to a historical encounter — a meeting with the Word of God. The Biblical understanding of the Word of God is that it is powerful. God's Word equals his action. In the Creation stories, God speaks and it is done. As Karl Barth has noted, the distinction we normally make between the actual and the theoretical does not exist with God. "In this centre of Christian faith the whole contrast, so current among us, between word and work, between knowing and living, ceases to have any meaning. But the Word, the *Logos,* is actually the work, the *ergon,* as well; the *verbum* is also the *opus.*"[86] God's Word creates community. This is the final, the ultimate ground of community. God's Word to man has been made manifest in specific historical events that form the nucleus of the Biblical message. These historic events bring into being the status community of the Word, the Israel of old, and the New Israel — the church. Our understanding of faith, then, is that it is an encounter with the Word of God made manifest in history, supremely in Jesus Christ. When this Word of God is encountered, something happens. Community is created and faith is elicited. Herein lies the importance of Dietrich Bonhoeffer's remark, "We are bound together by faith, not by experience."[87] What Bonhoeffer is stressing is that what binds Christians together into community is participation by way of faith in those objective events by which God has revealed himself in history, those events in which he has provided a meeting place with man. What unites us, then, is not our emotions, our feeling of good fellowship, but God's action. By faith we participate in that action and encounter God, are bound into community, and become men of faith. This is the "radical" type of faith that Clyde Holbrook speaks of as over against the probabilities of what he calls "primal" faith. "Radical faith is a continuing, conscious decision made by the self as a whole as it confronts the power, grace, and mystery of God. It is an act of existence, not of reason operating in isolation. Radical faith stands face to face with infidelity, meaninglessness, pride, and, in short, sin. It is not part of the continuum which runs from ignorance, through opinion and belief, to full knowledge." [88]

The Christian community, then, is the organic community of those who are justified by faith in God's activity in Jesus Christ. It is God's Word that creates this community wherein all men may participate by faith. This community is a status or an organic community where ethics, achievement, and human reason have a definite, significant, but not primary, place. It is the community where all moral imperatives rest upon the divine indicative—where the "Thou shalt" is seen in the relationship of God's action. It is the community where the stress is upon God's perfection and not man's. This community is a sacramental community where by means of symbolic rites men and women participate in those historic events which constitute the community of the body of Christ. Christian worship, which is primarily sacramental, is a reenactment of the drama of God's encounter with man through his Word. Through participation in this worship, Christians discover who they are as the sent people of God.

This Christian community is the primary community which does not necessitate the existence of competitive communities in order to be what it is. The other communities of men that have existed and will continue to exist are enveloped within the pervasiveness of the Christian community but not annulled or destroyed by it.

The communities that continue to exist beside the community of the church have, in Protestant theology, been thought of under headings of "the orders of creation." Dietrich Bonhoeffer refers to them as "the mandates." The mandates are under Christ, partaking of the realm of redemption, and are not just orders of creation. These mandates are the family, the state, the culture (the university being the primary cultural institution), and the church. All of these mandates invoke status relationships. Bonhoeffer notes that friendship and freedom are the root of culture—that is, of the university. But all of these "status" communities are in danger of being threatened by the encroachment of contractualism in our age. These communities need to support one another and to be seen in relationship to one another. It is possible that the church may conduct illicit relationships with the world.[89] What Bonhoeffer calls for is a true secularism which in order to be itself needs the church.

The question that now must be raised is the possibility, in a contractual society, of reestablishing the primacy of the status relationship. It is here that the church seems as much a captive of disintegrative forces as the culture in which it lives. There are, however, reasons for hope, a hope that may extend from the church to the other orders or mandates of society.

Chapter Nine

✠

The Renewal of Community

Many analyses of the Protestant Church today have been intensely critical, particularly of the institutional life of the denominations.[90] Writers note that there is little sense of Christian community, no distinctive Christian style of life, and weak sensitivity to mission. One might well conclude from these pessimistic reports that the church today is sick unto death. This might be the ground for the deepest despair, save for one thing. This is that the characteristic mode of the church's existence is death and resurrection. This theme, derived from its deepest theological foundations, is the determinative rhythm of the life of the Christian church.

If this is the case, then the task of the renewal of the life of the church must not be to attempt to prevent the church from dying, but to have it so die that it may be raised to newness of life again. Willem A. Visser 't Hooft has written, "Again and again the Church needs to be protected against the downward pull of its own life by which it becomes an end in itself and ceases to be the obedient servant of its Lord."[91] He reminds us that Calvin noted that the story of the church is the story of many resurrections and that this conception ought to be dominant in our thinking about the renewal of the church in our day.

The church as the body of Christ is called upon to suffer the same fate as the physical body of its Lord. This means that the hope of Christians is not for some success judged by worldly standards, but for the miracle of divine grace whereby God raises from the dead and creates out of nothing. The renewal of community in the church is possible just because it is the will of God, and not because of any hopeful human signs or heroic efforts on the part of Christians.

It cannot be the aim of the church to increase its community, its prestige or influence in the world; it must be the aim of the church to be obedient. God may increase the size of the church, or he may decrease it. In any case the church must live by the evangelical law that he who would save his life will lose it and he who loses his life for the sake of Christ will find it. This means that the church, as well as the individual Christian, must expect to find renewal only when it learns to give life for the life of the world. Then and only then will the renewal of community occur as it grows out of the sacrificial experience of self-giving and finds a repetition in the modern age of the community that was established by the cross.

The renewal of the community of the church, in the university and throughout the world, is dependent upon an increasing recognition that it must be a community of suffering. Karl Löwith has noted that the problem of human history is the problem of human suffering. He also notes that there are two possible responses to this problem, that of Prometheus, the rebel, or that of Christ, the suffering servant.[92] The rebel produces lonely heroism, frequently leading to cynicism and despair; the suffering servant establishes community. Christ's suffering on behalf of all mankind has established a universal community. The church today must learn how to be a community of suffering, not for its own sake, but for the world's. This is not because martyrdom is virtuous in itself or that suffering is to be consciously sought out. Rather, the fulfillment by the church of its task will inevitably provoke suffering.

All through history the life of the church has been pictured as a warfare. But it is not, as has been so frequently thought, a warfare *against* the world. Rather it is a warfare on behalf of the world against forces that have enslaved or would enslave the world. It is instructive to note that in the New Testament this warfare is conceived of as essentially defensive. The armament listed in Eph., ch. 6, is defensive. This would seem to suggest that when the church is being the church, it will be attacked, and its success depends solely upon its being faithful. Hence the frequently repeated command to " stand fast."

Two examples of this call to suffering may be cited from the academic community. We have stressed that education in our day is in danger of being degraded and enslaved in becoming merely a tool in the national defense or the research department for big business. The university, for the historical reasons we have noted, is very suspicious of ecclesiastical domination, but it is rather naïve about other forms of domination. Christians within the university, principally faculty and administrators, must seek to ally themselves with those forces in the university which are seeking to preserve the autonomy and integrity of the university. This is not always a popular cause. To be a gadfly on the academic rump of the university is unlikely to win acclaim. It may even call for sacrifice of promotion, job, friends. But the only way it can be done is if the Christians in the university are being upborne by the community of love that is standing fast in its service to the world. The " publish or perish " edicts of university administrations, which force faculty to neglect their teaching and the informal relationships with students which are such important parts of real education, may force sacrificial obedience from the Christian faculty member. Many, indeed, have paid and are paying a price for their conviction that they are called upon to teach, to involve themselves with students, and to speak out on some of the controversial topics of the day.

Another way of looking at the rhythm of death and resurrection as dominating the life of the church is in terms of the conception of the continuing reformation of the church. The Reformation of the sixteenth century was an episode in a church that must continue to reform. The historical Reformation was partial in its impact on Western culture. We have seen that it produced comparatively few changes in the conception of higher education.[93] Today Protestantism is called upon to continue its reformation in its view of the world, and to develop a positive view of the secular. Dietrich Bonhoeffer has maintained that only the Christian can be a true secularist. What this means for the Christian in the university and for the church's impact on higher education in our day has yet to be determined. But a dedication to the task of self-giving for the life of the university, on the part of Christians in higher education, could produce startling new developments. It is only through the sacrificial ministry of the redemptive community in the world that the natural communities can be freed to be themselves and not be deified or left to a cynical relativism.[94]

Renewals of the church as the community of faith have generally been based upon a rediscovery of the way the Word of God comes to us through the Scriptures. Renewals must begin here, since the Bible is the record of the only true renewal ever to transpire, the renewal in Christ. New beginnings is a basic Biblical theme and the Genesis story is reiterated time and again in the New Testament. The dove at Jesus' baptism is the creative spirit of God that hovered like a dove over the chaotic abyss. The Prologue of John's Gospel begins with the opening words of Genesis. Paul treats of Jesus as the New Adam, and the book of The Revelation is based upon the seven days of the Creation story.[95] The Bible is the story of the creation of community by God, extending from Israel through the new Israel of the church to the final Kingdom of God.

Two basic criteria of renewal will then be those found in Scripture. The first is shared experience in the Word. The Bible must be studied, understood, taught, so that the Word may be heard. The sacraments must be shared, as they are the Word made visible. Secondly, there must be shared experience in the world. This is the experience of mission, which does not follow Bible study but accompanies it. Only as a Christian is sharing in mission can he understand what the Word is that is being spoken to him.[96]

To be put under the discipline of studying the Word and to participate in the sacraments of the church is to be made into a fellowship by the Word of God. To be engaged in the ministry of mission in the world is to share the fellowship of Christ's suffering and to be knit together in the bond of the ministry of the Suffering Servant. There is no other way to find a renewal of the church. It is these experiences which build Christian community, though this is not their primary purpose. There are no shortcuts or Rotary Club versions of this type of community. It is tragic that the church frequently has to be driven to this discipline only through shattering disappointments and failures.

The challenge to the Christian community within the

university is to provide an open community where true education can take place. By doing this, the church would be providing the greatest service to the university. Suzanne de Dietrich has said that "our firm belief is that it is part of the calling of the church to show the world what true community means: a fellowship of free persons bound to one another by a common calling and a common service. Only in Christ can we solve the tension between freedom and authority, between the right of the individual person to attain fullness of life and the claim of the community as a whole on each of its members. For in and through him we learn what it means to be perfectly free, yet obedient unto death; to come as a servant, yet through this very self-abasement to attain fullness of life."[97]

Thus the Christians in the university must become a community by gathering around the Word and must also serve as a community scattered and involved in the whole life of the university, or their witness will be isolated and irrelevant. The issue is quite simple, but obedience is difficult. Visser 't Hooft says: "'Be ye renewed' does not mean: 'Get busy and find some different and better method of Christian action.' It means: 'Expose yourself to the life-giving work of God. Pray that he may make the dry bones come to life. Expect great things from him. And get ready to do what he commands.'"[98]

Appendix One

✠

The Place of Community in American Colleges

AMERICAN HIGHER EDUCATION has always manifested a concern for community but has experienced a gradual divorce of community from the principal issue in education — that is, from the learning process. American education is a combination of one factor from continental education and one factor from British education. The British pattern of education, as represented by the universities of Oxford and Cambridge, is residential and tutorial. The student, living in a college, is related to a tutor who is in charge of his educational experience. The emphasis of education is on the tutorial relationship rather than on examinations or lectures. Continental education, on the other hand, has the tradition of not providing living units for the students, and the classroom-lecture method predominates. The early American universities were modeled after the British pattern; however, in the nineteenth century the continental pattern began to dominate. It may be argued that American education took the wrong factor from British education and the wrong factor from continental education. If American education had continued to be centered around a strong tutorial system and had put the amount of money that has been put into residences into increasing the number and quality of faculty, commuting education — the dominant form of modern education — might be academically more significant today.

The rise of the fraternity system in America has paralleled the increasing individualism and impersonality of the educational process. The attempt is to provide community in relationship to education. But rather than being supportive of the essential academic task, fraternity community life has, in fact, tended to detract from it. One might speculate that there might be a possibility of redeeming the fraternity system by relating it to the central academic task. There is also the possibility of developing a commuting tutorial type of education to meet the needs for changing student values and for creating community around the essential academic task of education. But there is little evidence that such proposals are likely to be taken seriously by fraternities or educators.

Appendix Two

✠

An Illustrative Biblical Study

In what is really a continuous work, Luke-Acts, we find the first attempt at a Christian historiography. The writer endeavors to demonstrate how the clue to the meaning of history is brought to a focus in the city of Jerusalem in the life, death, and resurrection of Jesus and how this focus then expands from Jerusalem in the mission of the infant church, culminating in the arrival of Paul in the city of Rome.

The book commonly known as The Acts of the Apostles might better have been termed The Acts of the Holy Spirit. For it is the Holy Spirit who is the chief agent of the missionary expansion of the church. This work contains many examples of what we have called "unstructured mission," but perhaps none is more instructive for the mission of the church on the campus than the incident of the conversion of Cornelius in the tenth chapter. Even a cursory examination of this chapter with a little imagination is sufficient to show how filled with relevant material for the campus ministry is this strange incident.

Acts 10:1-8. Cornelius, a God-fearer, is being prepared for the mission of the church even before he comes into contact with Christians. The Holy Spirit as Lord of the mission of the church is engaged in preparing for the witness of the Christian community. We may therefore expect that God is at work in the world and on the campus even where Christians least expect it, to prepare the way for the coming of the word of witness.

Acts 10:9-23. Peter's religious experience on the rooftop of the sheet coming down from heaven filled with all kinds of animals was initially not understood by him. But rather than staying on the rooftop until he fully understood, he obeyed and went on an embassy to Cornelius, not knowing fully what he was letting himself in for, nor having a clearly formulated theology as to what he was doing. Certainly this is a clear example of "unstructured mission." This would seem to indicate that preparation for the mission of the church on the campus need not involve any great theological maturity or the arming of the Christian witness with a completely watertight system with all the answers. What is required to be involved in mission is obedience, openness to the form this mission may take, and faith that the Holy Spirit is preparing the way. The theology will only become clear, as Peter found, when one in obedience actually involves himself in mission.

Acts 10:23. It is also significant that this embassy of Peter's was a mission of the Christian community. Peter was accompanied by other members of the church. Wherever the church is engaged in mission it ought to be a matter of a Christian fellowship and not a go-it-alone endeavor.

Acts 10:26. Peter's humility in refusing the obeisance of Cornelius reveals his willingness to stand beside other men as a man. He demonstrates a solidarity with the world — a refusal to draw attention to self which all too infrequently has characterized the church's mission.

Acts 10:27-47. The results of Peter's preaching were

wholly unexpected. The Holy Spirit fell on Cornelius and his friends. But the change was not only in them. Peter and his fellow Christians were also changed. Peter saw at once the relevancy of his puzzling rooftop vision, and the universality of the gospel was driven home in the minds of these Christians of Jewish origin. In an experience of true evangelism the evangelist is also evangelized. Something happens to the witness as well as those to whom he witnesses. Unfortunately the mission of the church has frequently been thought of in terms of those who have giving to those who have not, or those who have changed trying to get others to become as they are. But evangelism is rather, as D. T. Niles has noted, more like one beggar telling another beggar where they may both find bread.

We must also recall that the change in Peter was not permanent. He reverted to his former exclusive position when he returned to the Jerusalem church and had to be reprimanded by Paul, as we read in Gal. 2:11. This reminds us that we must not expect that Christians will always wholeheartedly respond to the bidding of the Spirit. Often they have to be reconverted again and again. Patience must continually be practiced by those whose insights, like those of Paul, are clearer and more consistent.

Acts 10:48. Peter and his fellow Christians adapted themselves to the realities of the situation. Previously the Holy Spirit had been given only to those already baptized. But here was positive evidence that the Holy Spirit was present before baptism. Peter did not insist that the evidence be denied, rather, he sought to regularize what had happened as best he could. Baptism was performed after the gift of the Spirit. This certainly suggests that the church ought not to seek to impose its expectations, even those based on long experience, upon its missionary experience. The church must adopt whatever forms or structures will make its response to the missionary activity of the Holy Spirit creative and obedient.

If the insights of this single chapter are applied to the understanding of the mission of the church on the campus, then it becomes obvious that it is not the task of the church "to carry Christ on campus." Rather, the task of the church is to go out and meet him on the campus where he is already reigning in judgment and mercy, preparing the way for the witness of the Christian. The task of the community of faith is not to take Christ into the world, but to identify him who is to be met in his world so that the world may know who its Lord is. This necessitates involvement in the whole life of the world—or of the campus by those who have learned the signs of God's activity and who are willing to follow his example by giving their lives for the life of the world.

✠

Notes

1. The term "culture" is used in its widest sense, including technology, law, politics, and customs, not in the narrow sense of aesthetics.

2. See an early work on the campus ministry by Clarence Shedd, *The Church Follows Its Students* (Yale University Press, 1938).

3. See the article by Reinhold Niebuhr, "The Two Sources of Western Culture," in *The Christian Idea of Education,* ed. by Edmund Fuller (Yale University Press, 1957). In this article Niebuhr also states some reasons for the gradual supremacy of the Hellenistic elements in the synthesis. In the same work another article, by William G. Pollard, "Dark Age and Renaissance in the Twentieth Century," indicates signs of an increasing capacity in our culture to respond to Hebraic aspects of culture. Such a renaissance would assist the theological and academic dialogue.

4. Not until 1879 did Leo XIII endorse Thomism as the official standard for Roman Catholic theology.

5. See Jarislav Pelikan, *Human Culture and the Holy* (SCM Press, Ltd., London, 1955), for a thorough treatment of what is summarized here.

6. Paul Tillich today makes use of the same argument.

7. Hegel is the supreme example of this identification.

8. Dietrich Bonhoeffer strongly rejected this dependence upon man's extremity or weakness as providing a "space" for theology. Cf. *Prisoner for God* (The Macmillan Company, 1954), p. 159.

9. H. Richard Niebuhr, *Christ and Culture* (Faber & Faber, Ltd., London, 1952).

10. *Ibid.*, p. 69.

11. *Ibid.*, p. 110.

12. *Ibid.*, p. 145.

13. For a detailed critique, see Emil Brunner, *The Divine Imperative* (The Westminster Press, 1947), pp. 626 ff.

14. H. Richard Niebuhr, *op. cit.*, p. 188.

15. Dietrich Bonhoeffer, *Ethics* (The Macmillan Company, 1955), p. 64.

16. I am indebted to Dr. Benjamin Reist, of San Francisco Theological Seminary, for his penetrating insights on the relevance of Troeltsch's work for an understanding of Bonhoeffer.

17. Ernst Troeltsch, *The Social Teaching of the Christian Churches,* Volumes I and II (Harper & Row, Publishers, Inc., 1960).

18. This is not a comment unique to Bonhoeffer; cf. Nicolas Berdyaev, *The Beginning and the End* (Harper & Row, Publishers, Inc., 1957), p. 12.

19. Bonhoeffer, *op. cit.*, p. 31.

20. "The task of the Church is without parallel. The *corpus Christianum* is broken asunder. The *corpus Christi* confronts a hostile world. The world has known Christ and has turned its back on Him, and it is to this world that the Church must now prove that Christ is the living Lord. Even while she waits for the last day, the Church, as the bearer of an historical inheritance, is bound by an obligation to the historical future." *Ibid.*, pp. 44–45.

21. See Ch. IX.

22. It is also noteworthy that such experiments in the lay ministry as Kirkridge and the Faith and Life Community in Austin, Texas, are independent rather than officially denominational in character. Even Parishfield, solely an Episcopalian operation initially, has become interdenominational in its operations.

23. E.g., Jacques Ellul, Willem A. Visser 't Hooft, Hendrik Kraemer, etc.

24. T. W. Manson, *The Church's Ministry* (The Westminster Press, 1948), p. 23.

25. William J. Wolf, *Man's Knowledge of God* (Doubleday & Company, Inc., 1955), pp. 132–133.

26. Cf. Wolf-Deiter Marsh, "The Church in Society," in *Student World* (World's Student Christian Federation, Geneva, 1959), No. 1.

27. Paul L. Lehmann, "The Foundation and Pattern of Chris-

tian Behavior," in *Christian Faith and Social Action,* ed. by John A. Hutchison (Charles Scribner's Sons, 1953), p. 108 (italics mine).

28. Cf. Markus Barth, *The Broken Wall: A Study of the Epistle to the Ephesians* (Judson Press, 1959).

29. Cf. the works of Dietrich Bonhoeffer, Arnold Toynbee, Herbert Butterfield, Karl Löwith, etc.

30. Karl Heim, "Christian Faith and the Growing Power of Secularism," in *Religion and Culture,* ed. by Walter Leibrecht (Harper & Row, Publishers, Inc., 1959), p. 194.

31. George Williams, *Wilderness and Paradise in Christian Thought* (Harper & Row, Publishers, Inc., 1962), pp. 168 ff.

32. For a detailed history of the university, see Hastings Rashdall, *The Universities of Europe in the Middle Ages* (Clarendon Press, Oxford, 1895), and Isaac L. Kandel, *History of Secondary Education* (Houghton Mifflin Company, 1930).

33. See the dominance of this idea in Karl Jaspers, *The Idea of the University* (Beacon Press, Inc., 1959).

34. The Ecclesiastical Ordinances of 1541 stated that "a college should be instituted for instructing children to prepare them for the ministry as well as for civil government."

35. Frederick Eby, *The Development of Modern Education* (Prentice-Hall, Inc., 1952), p. 117.

36. The material on curriculum development in American colleges was collected by Dr. Neil Warren, Dean of the College of Letters, Arts, and Sciences of the University of Southern California, as part of a preparatory study for a major curriculum revision in that school.

37. Sir Walter Moberly, *The Crisis in the University* (SCM Press, Ltd., London, 1949), pp. 43 ff.

38. The studies, analyses, projections, and statistics in the area of higher education are too numerous to list. Those persons desiring to keep abreast of developments here may subscribe to the material published by the American Council on Education, 785 Massachusetts Avenue, N.W., Washington, D.C., 20006.

39. Cf. David Riesman, *The Lonely Crowd* (Yale University Press, 1956). David Riesman has noted that humanities courses for engineering students provide little more than the possibility for the technically trained engineer to carry on a conversation at a cocktail party. Riesman suggests that humanities for those in the field of sciences occupy the same position that the classics did for British

civil servants in the nineteenth century, largely irrelevant but highly valued.

40. Max Wise, *They Come for the Best of Reasons: College Students Today* (American Council on Education, 1958).

41. *General Education in a Free Society: Report of the Harvard Committee* (Harvard University Press, 1945).

42. Harold K. Schilling, *The University and the Church* (Department of Campus Christian Life, United Church of Christ, 1955), p. 3.

43. John Calvin, *Institutes of the Christian Religion,* ed. by John T. McNeill; tr. and indexed by Ford Lewis Battles (The Westminster Press, 1960), I.i.

44. Cf. Arthur Schlesinger, Jr., "The One Against the Many," in *Saturday Review,* July 14, 1962, in which the danger of ideologies, including theological ideologies, is clearly noted.

45. Along this line, see Dietrich Bonhoeffer's poem "Who Am I?" in *Prisoner for God* (The Macmillan Company, 1954), p. 165.

46. The theme of the death of God and the death of man is of course a long and significant one in Western thought, not being restricted merely to authorized theological circles.

47. It is significant here that in the Bible we have no one view of Jesus Christ, but four Gospels each presenting somewhat significantly divergent understandings of the role and person of Jesus, supplemented also by the writings of Paul and the highly poetic and divergent images in the book of The Revelation.

48. One of the most popular of these was once referred to by a speaker at a higher education conference as "no Christ, but a bearded Horatio Alger"!

49. Cf. J. Courtney Murray, "The Making of a Pluralistic Society," in *Religion and the University,* ed. by Erich A. Walter (University of Michigan Press, 1958), p. 17.

50. Marjorie Reeves, *Three Questions in Higher Education* (The Edward W. Hazen Foundation, 1955), p. 14.

51. In an unpublished lecture, Temple University, fall, 1959.

52. For an interesting exposition of differing views of man, see *What Is the Nature of Man? Images of Man in Our American Culture,* by Kenneth Boulding and others (Christian Education Press, 1959).

53. Along this line, see Alexander Miller's *The Man in the Mirror* (Doubleday & Company, Inc., 1958).

54. It is here that Tillich's Protestant Principle is such a relevant concept.

55. Herbert Butterfield, *Christianity and History* (Charles Scribner's Sons, 1949), p. 146.

56. W. A. Visser 't Hooft and J. H. Oldham, *The Church and Its Functions in Society* (Allen & Unwin, Ltd., London, 1937), pp. 209–210.

57. Moberly, *op. cit.*; A. J. Coleman, *The Task of the Christian in the University* (Association Press, 1947).

58. Robert M. Hutchins with Joseph P. Lyford, *A Conversation: The Political Animal* (Fund for the Republic, Inc., Center for the Study of Democratic Institutions, 1962), p. 18.

59. John H. Newman, *The Idea of a University* (Longmans, Green & Co., Ltd., London, 1912); Jaspers, *op. cit.*

60. *Ibid.*, p. ix.

61. *Ibid.*, p. 118.

62. Cf. David Riesman, *Constraint and Variety in American Education* (Doubleday & Company, Inc., 1958), pp. 113–114.

63. Marjorie Reeves, *op. cit.*, pp. 6–7.

64. Here we have Paul Tillich's concern for ontological courage — the courage to be. Without it man cannot grasp the total situation. See *The Courage to Be* (Yale University Press, 1952).

65. Phillip E. Jacob, *Changing Values in College* (The Edward W. Hazen Foundation, 1956).

66. Dr. William Poteat, of Duke University, recalls a brilliant student who did a particularly poor job on a paper on Kierkegaard. After counseling the student it became obvious that her problem was a social one. When this problem began to be cleared up, her understanding of Kierkegaard improved remarkably. The point was that in her lonely and exposed condition she could not afford to really understand Kierkegaard because of the threat he presented her.

67. Schilling, *op. cit.*

68. Marjorie Reeves, *op. cit.*, pp. 18 ff. Miss Reeves mentions the relevance of the Christian faith to her role of teacher of history in noting that her faith safeguards, on theological grounds, the intractability of the material with which she deals. It also sets limits to the knowability at the human level and forces her to recognize the element of mystery that eludes our grasp in all intellectual analyses.

69. The issue of community is to this extent like the problem of

an American national purpose. A Presidential committee was set up a few years ago to discover and delineate national goals. This only happens when there is little awareness of these goals in society at large.

70. Clyde Holbrook, *Faith and Community* (Harper & Row, Publishers, Inc., 1959).

71. *Ibid.,* p. 111.

72. *Ibid.*

73. *Ibid.*

74. "Man cannot be man 'by himself'; he can only be man in community. For love can only operate in community, and only in this operation of love is man human." *Ibid.*

75. *Ibid.,* pp. 111–112.

76. Harry R. Davis and Robert C. Good, *Reinhold Niebuhr on Politics* (Charles Scribner's Sons, 1960), p. 100.

77. Note Dietrich Bonhoeffer's strong liturgical emphasis in *Life Together* (Harper & Row, Publishers, Inc., 1954).

78. See the works of Hayakawa and Korzibski.

79. Another way of looking at the determinative aspect of history may be seen in terms of Richard Niebuhr's distinction between "inner history" and "outer history." Outer history is history about which we can be impartial or relatively so, whereas inner history is that history which has made us what we are and in which we are existentially involved. For Americans, the distinction would be between the history of the Ming dynasty in China (outer history) and that of the Revolution of 1776 (inner history).

80. A somewhat similar analysis to Demant's has been made by the English sociologist Main. Anthropologists such as Margaret Mead and psychoanalysts such as Eric Fromm have worked out similar themes contrasting Apollonarian and Dionysian cultures or mother love and the paternal type of affection.

81. The role of ceremonies in the creation of such a status relationship as friendship is poignantly presented in the experience of the taming of the little fox in Antoine Saint-Exupéry's *The Little Prince* (Reynal & Hitchcock, 1943).

82. Paul Tillich, "Our Unchristian World," in *Man's Disorder and God's Design* (The Amsterdam Assembly Series, World Council of Churches, 1949), p. 61.

83. Reinhold Niebuhr, *The Nature and Destiny of Man* (Charles Scribner's Sons, 1948), pp. 67–68.

84. Arnold Toynbee, *The World and the West* (Oxford University Press, 1953), p. 96.

85. L. S. Thornton, *The Common Life in the Body of Christ* (The Dacre Press, London, 1942), p. 51.

86. Karl Barth, *Dogmatics in Outline* (Harper & Row, Publishers, Inc., 1959), p. 67.

87. Bonhoeffer, *Life Together,* p. 39.

88. Holbrook, *op. cit.,* p. 38.

89. See The Book of Hosea.

90. See Gibson Winter, *The Suburban Captivity of the Churches* (Doubleday & Company, Inc., 1961), and Peter Berger, *The Noise of Solemn Assemblies* (Doubleday & Company, Inc., 1961).

91. Willem A. Visser 't Hooft, *The Renewal of the Church* (The Westminster Press, 1956), p. 68.

92. Karl Löwith, *Meaning in History* (The University of Chicago Press, 1949), p. 3.

93. Emil Brunner, *op. cit.* In this work Brunner notes that the Reformation was never applied to the field of ethics at all. It was not until 1932 that an evangelical ethic was written.

94. Cf. Heim, *op. cit.*

95. Austin Farrer, *A Rebirth of Images* (The Dacre Press, London, 1949).

96. See Appendix Two.

97. Suzanne de Dietrich, *The Witnessing Community* (The Westminster Press, 1958), pp. 13–14.

98. Visser 't Hooft, *op. cit.,* pp. 90–91.